Eight lively children running in and about the parsonage often add up to charming chaos, complete with hilarious tricks, mischievous pranks, embarrassing scenes, *and* many tender moments. Here is a behind-the-scenes glimpse through the all-revealing eyes of the youngest daughter in Papa's big family. Read about courtships carried on behind Papa's back, little Paul's intense fear of the holy "ghost," the bride who lost her petticoat, and many other irresistibly human and humorous events. From the first chapter to the last, here is a warm and witty picture of a father adored by his children and of a wonderful family life in an American parsonage.

Papa Was a Preacher

ALYENE PORTER

Illustrated by JANET SMALLEY

SPIRE BOOKS

Fleming H. Revell Company
Old Tappan, New Jersey

ISBN-0-8007-8350

A Spire Book

Published by Spire Books,
A Division of Fleming H. Revell Company,
Old Tappan, New Jersey

TO my mother

CONTENTS

Preface

A MAIDEN lady of my acquaintance has placed on the wall over her desk a framed inscription for the edification of those who are condescendingly sorry that she is unmarried. It reads:

> THE REGRET OVER WHAT I HAVE MISSED IS SWALLOWED UP IN THE RELIEF AT WHAT I HAVE ESCAPED

That is how we feel about having grown up in a parsonage. Its restricted atmosphere has meant missing some things, but the shelter of its dignity has meant escape from other things.

And love was there, and truth, and laughter.

What more can life hold?

WHEN I told Papa of my plan to write this book, he said, "Sh-h-h-h! If you do that, I'll have to quit preaching." So in taking out some of the family skeletons I have hastily shoved two or three back into the closet and slammed the door. Even so, I submit these pages with fear and trembling—that in the family gallery there will be one photograph with its face turned against the wall. That will be mine.

ALYENE PORTER

Go and Preach

PAPA was a preacher. Papa is still a preacher—as true to his convictions as the day he gave his pipe a final fling into a cornfield and entered the pulpit. Since that day he has never taken a backward look into the oblivion to which he consigned the pipe but has "pressed toward the mark for the prize of the high calling." He has nodded to the progress of civilization only when it has involved a superficial change and disturbed not a whit his religious roots. His outward yielding is reflected in the wearing of vestments by his choir and the promptness with which he closes each service, but the rock of faith from which he delivers his sermons is the same on which he took his stand forty years ago, and the gospel that resounds through the rafters still rings with the old-time religion.

In his youth Papa did not plan to preach. He hitched

his wagon to a more terrestrial star. "I'll be the most
prosperous landowner in Mississippi," he said to himself. But there is an Eastern proverb which says, "A
fig tree looking on a fig tree beareth fruit." So Papa,
looking on his preacher father, began to bear fruit for
the ministry unknowingly. Lending eyesight to his
blinded father that he might finish his work, Papa
began to hear a still small voice saying, "Go . . . and
preach!"

Papa did not want to preach. "No," he protested.
"I'll teach school until I can buy a farm. I'll accumulate land, build a magnificent house, marry, and live in
one place the rest of my life."

In his mind the path of teaching led to all other
roads. That was understandable. His mother, who died
at his birth, had been a teacher; his father had stepped
from teaching into the ministry; and every adult rela-
tive on either side of the family could be located on
pedagogical route—among them Papa's cousin John,
president of the Teacher's Institute in Chalybeate
Springs, Mississippi. It was there that Papa planned to
don his academic robes.

During the summer before his entry, however, des-
tiny stalked across his path in the form of Uncle Ben,
who was moving "out West."

"Edwin," he hailed Papa one day. "how would you
like to guide my immigrant car to Texas and stay with
us till school starts?"

Papa's joy was unconfined. His mental picture of
Texas was of the usual exaggerated contour—that it
was a vast expanse roamed by wild animals and inhab-
ited by supermen with spurs on their boots, six-
shooters on their hips, and evil in their hearts. Papa

felt like Livingstone going to Darkest Africa.

According to the custom of those migrating west, Uncle Ben chartered a freight car for moving. In one end were stacked household goods and farm implements, while the other sheltered the horses and dogs. (Nobody ever moved a cow to Texas!) Between the ends, eight feet of space provided the luxurious traveling compartment by day for the "guide"—in this case, Papa. It was his duty to feed the animals, for which a trough was built on the side of the car, to present when necessary the contract proving the legality of the equipage, and to see that it was switched and coupled to the right trains—after which he could stretch his limbs for a long night's rest in the caboose.

And thus it happened that after three days of guiding an immigrant car, Papa leveled his gaze to behold, not the expected maze of jungle, but a beautiful prairie carpeted with green and garnished with sunshine. It looked to him like the Promised Land! Then and there Papa became a devoted son of the motherly Lone Star State. In jubilation he cried, "She's just like the old woman who lived in the shoe—with so much land she doesn't know what to do." And Papa wanted land—land to accumulate, land to cultivate, land to love.

He made a cactus-by-cactus inspection of the state that summer and traveled back to Mississippi only to count the days until he could again raise his eyes to a Texas sky.

On the first day at Teachers' Institute as he was strolling out of the main building, his mind filled with a dream of Texas, Papa's reverie was broken by a more

dazzling vision. When Pearl Wilson swished by him
and rounded the corner, Papa's heart bounded after
her in ardent pursuit. But she gave no evidence that
she was aware of his existence. As she sat at the dor-
mitory supper table that evening, however, she must
have heard the eager thumping of a heart near by, for
she turned sparkling brown eyes straight into Papa's.

"Yes," she said, "I hope to be here the full two
years. I'm studying to be an elocution teacher."

But already Papa was mapping out another career
for her. "Chalybeate Springs Institute," he would say
reminiscently to us when we were young, "that's
where I found your mother."

"But, Father," she would protest, "I was never
lost!"

Pressed for the truth, however, she would admit that
from that first day her dreams were colored by the
vision of the tall, blue-eyed cousin of "Prexy."

Dates were strictly forbidden by the cousinly president; but Papa, like that other Romeo, stoutly declared, "What love can do that dares love attempt;
. . . kinsmen are no let to me." And Mother, like the
other Juliet, gloried in his daring.

That "bud of love, by summer's ripening breath"
became indeed a "beauteous flower." Another year of
learning, another spring, then the joyful wedding bells
pealed forth, and in the fall, Papa proudly carried his
happy bride across a Texas threshold.

DISPENSING reading, writing, and arithmetic in a country school, still dreaming of acres of diamonds, Papa
again heard the still small voice, "Go . . . and
preach!"

But Papa did not want to preach! Like Jacob he wrestled with the angel. "I can't preach," he said. "I wouldn't know what to say. And besides I'd be embarrassed telling people how they should live!"

Mother was conscious of his inner struggle. One day while reading Emerson she quoted aloud, "Does he lack organ or medium to impart his truth? He can still fall back on this elemental force of living them." She closed the book. "You don't have to be a great orator to be a good preacher, Edwin," she said reassuringly. "You could just *live* your religion."

The following Sunday a visiting minister preached at their small chapel. He chose as his text, "I am not ashamed of the Gospel of Christ." To Papa it seemed that only the two of them were present—he and the minister—as straightforward eyes gazed steadily into his and a pleading voice said again and again, "I AM NOT ASHAMED OF THE GOSPEL OF CHRIST! I AM NOT ASHAMED OF THE GOSPEL OF CHRIST! *I am not ashamed . . .*"

On the way home, Papa broke the heavy silence. "I'm going to be a preacher!" he told Mother in tones of sheer joy.

"Thank God, my dear!" she said. "And I will help you."

PAPA's first assignment in the new life was the serving of six rural churches. On horseback he traveled to the six points on his "circuit." Since that time, for forty years he has voiced the Gospel to Texans in rural chapel, in small-town church, and in city temple.

From those first years he has obeyed the literal law of his beliefs. In rearing eight children Papa has never

found it necessary to buy on Sunday. Feed for his circuit-riding horse was bought on Saturday; gasoline for his car is still bought on Saturday. Even ice and milk for Sunday were delivered the night before. We usually kept a cow, but once when we were without one, Papa opened a sleepy eye on Sunday morning to see the milk ordered for Saturday night being placed on the doorstep. He went to the telephone.

"Mrs. Brown," he kindly addressed the wife of the dairyman-farmer, "I'm sorry. We don't buy milk on Sunday."

"But, Brother Porter," came her incredulous protest, "unfortunately the cows *give* milk on Sunday."

"Yes," sighed Papa in regretful tone, "unfortunately!"

Papa literally tries to "do unto others." In the early years riding along country roads in his buggy, he offered a ride to every traveler along the way. Today,

with danger from hitchhikers upon the highway, he yet invites every pedestrian to share his car—and with never a mishap.

In the early years, one night a bolt of lightning struck the corner of the living room, where Papa sat with three friends playing dominoes. It shocked the four of them and set fire to the house. "It was a judgment of God," was Papa's interpretation, as with one broad gesture he committed the dominoes to the open fire. "Never again shall a domino, deck of cards, or any such appearance of evil enter my house." And they never did.

In these and many other ways Papa has been exacting of himself and of his family in upholding the right and suppressing the wrong, as he saw it. A father is to be obeyed. We respected his judgment and obeyed his wishes as a matter of course. But it was never through fear. How could a little girl fear a father who patiently laced her shoes in the morning, took her "pastoral" visiting with him during the day, and lovingly tucked her into bed at night?

Fierce for the right, he bore his part
    In strife with many a valiant foe;
But laughter winged his polished dart,
    and kindness tempered every blow.

Papa's innate kindness and his exterior cover of
modernness are slightly misleading to his grandchildren. Though his rigidity is apparent to any adult, his
grandchildren take a matter-of-fact attitude toward his
preaching and adopt a freedom in bossing him which
his children would never dare exercise.

One Sunday a grandson, three years old, was in the
congregation. It was nearing twelve o'clock, and the
attentive stillness was broken only by the sound of
Papa's voice, preaching earnestly.

Suddenly Paul stood upon the pew. He raised a
commanding little hand and a more commanding little
voice. "Granddaddy," he called out, "that will be
about enough."

Papa forced a cough, then openly abandoned himself
to a grin. "We will close the service," he said, "by
singing 'Praise God from whom all blessings flow.' "

As we sang the words, "Praise Father, Son, and
Holy Ghost," it set me reminiscing about the time
when Paul's father, the baby of our family, firmly sat in
his little rocker one Sunday night and refused to go to
church. When Mother urged his reason, he said, "I'm
afraid of the Holy Ghost."

And as I delved into the past, I realized how colored
with hymns, prayers, and clerical terminology was all
of our thinking and speaking, during those years when
eight of us were stretching the walls of a Methodist
parsonage with our growing, our merriment, and our

off-the-pastoral-record escapades.

We are long since grown and scattered. But the color of those years in the life picture of each of us is more vivid than all the splashes of adult years—that time of life when we were being reared to full estate by a mother whose memory is a vibration of heavenly music and a father who exuded from his pulpit and in his home a Herculean strength of character linked with a childlike simplicity of faith and gentleness.

Perhaps we fitted into the timeworn pattern cut to make us the worst children in town. But "all God's chillun" have impulses; and since preachers' children spend three-fourths of their time in church, those impulses have to be expressed there and observed by the greatest number of people.

No preacher's child can ever have a feeling of anonymity. Even now, as a woman, when I walk into a strange church two thousand miles from home I can feel eyes directed toward me and hear a whispered echo, "That's the preacher's youngest daughter." And from that moment every move must befit such a niche in life.

The concentrated light from many eyes forms a giant spotlight to illuminate the on-stage actions of ministers' children, while in the comparative darkness outside the spotlight identical actions of other children go unnoticed. To function always within the focus of an all-seeing eye naturally prompts daring action and a reckless determination to give a show worth the looking at. With a cast of eight characters of varying ages and temperaments, the gallery watching our show was assured of a new bill each week.

THE oldest of the troupe was Hugh. When he was four if Mother let a single day pass without drilling him stiffly on the three *R's* Papa reproached her for letting the child grow up in ignorance. Philosophical and quiet from his first years, he could always be depended upon to retrieve the family dignity when it was lost by a younger member. His ambition was to become a bishop.

Two years younger was Cecil, taciturn but mischievous. Early in life, he decided to be a financier and take care of the artistic, impractical members of the clan. At the age of twelve, by saving the money he had earned delivering groceries and sweeping the church, he had accumulated the sum of fifty dollars. In our circumstances it was unheard of to have that much cash at one time. One day in sending Cecil's suit to the cleaner, Papa discovered the gold mine and was overcome with grief that his son should have stepped from the path of honesty. Cecil had to explain hastily that quarter by quarter, dollar by dollar, he had tucked the money away over a period of two years.

The thirdling was Raybon, the family's Don Juan. On his fifth birthday, he came into the house crying bitterly. When Mother sympathetically coaxed him to give words to his grief, he wailed, "I'm five today! I'm getting so old; but I don't want to get married, and I don't want to be an old bachelor. So what can I do?"

By his twelfth year, however, the idea of marriage had triumphed, and from that time his fancy lightly turned to thoughts of love. At fourteen his dates were so numerous that Papa had to forbid them under threat of punishment. Raybon went serenely on, dating as usual. And Papa did not spare the rod. With a this-hurts-me-worse-than-it-hurts-you tone he asked, "Son, why do you deliberately disobey me?"

"Well, Papa," Raybon replied, "I thought it over and decided that I'd rather take the punishment than miss seeing the girls."

As the years advanced, much of the time which Papa might have devoted to composing eloquent sermons was spent getting Raybon disengaged from the girls to whom he became engaged. A golden-voiced soloist who could play the piano and had a way with him, he was irresistible and unresisting. And when during revival meetings he sang, "Come to the Mercy Seat," the seat became immediately and completely peopled with romantic girls. "Verily he hath his reward." His days are now blessed with a lovely wife and three daughters.

Edd was the next in line. Solid, dependable, always loving, he was Mother's first assistant—in cooking, housekeeping, and taking care of the younger children. His familiarity with the preparation of meals for ten was probably responsible for his ambition to become a wholesale grocery merchant.

The four boys so near the same age composed a quartet of noise and prankishness equal to anything short of dynamite. When they were two, four, six and eight years old they decided they were tired of going to church—and promptly crawled under the church building to set it on fire. When the blaze was discovered and extinguished, with small loss, no little boys were visible, and it was conceded that the fire was of unexplained origin. The next Sunday saw the four sitting piously in their accustomed pew.

The masculine trend of the family was finally bro-

ken, and with great jubilation, one day the boys
learned that they had a sister. Janette became the family musician. Though she was never the official church
organist, from the time she was ten she had to be on
time for every service and ready to play if the regular
organist felt disposed to be absent. She would also
sing, pray, or tend babies as the occasion demanded.
When she was fourteen and away at Epworth League
Conference, she wrote home that she had consecrated
her life as a missionary and was going to China. I was
inconsolable in the belief that she was going straight to
China, to be swallowed whole by a cannibal, and that I
should never look on my sister's face again. Mother
explained that she would be with us a while longer, at
least until she finished her education. At twenty she
fell in love, married, and is still with us.

The feminine trend of the family was short-lived.
Two years later there was another boy, Gilderoy. He
entered the world with a clinical eye, and from that
time on, in his own fashion, he practiced medicine. He
prescribed his own remedy for every kind of ill of
mankind. He made our perfectly healthy dogs and cats
go through life with splints on their legs, and he lived
with the burning desire to become a great surgeon.

It was then my turn to make an appearance, which I
did slightly before the right cue—completely disrupt-
ing one of Papa's revival meetings away from home.
Consistent with such a dramatic beginning, I yearned
to be an actress and was always in character, deigning
to give the family only an occasional glimpse of the
real me. It was so effective in calling to one of the
brothers to say, "Hist, Romeo!"—or on going to bed,

"Call me early, Mother dear, for I'm to be Queen o' the May." I marked time by giving recitations on Sunday-school programs, only until the cloak of the great Sarah Bernhardt should fall upon my shoulders.

We were all blessed with perfect health, but when I was two, a little brother was born who was never well and who died at the age of five months. It was the first shadow to fall on our home, and although for the rest of her life Mother had eight active children, she always remembered that Bryan Barton's place was vacant.

Two and a half years later Paul Candler was born. To ensure his success in life he was named for the Apostle Paul and Bishop Candler. As he was the only redhead in a family of brunettes his nicknames were legion—"Strawberry," "Pinkie," "Red," "Huckleberry Finn," and "Freckles."

The rest of us envied his total lack of inhibitions. He never restrained an impulse. His flaming hair was companioned by vivid freckles vying for standing space on his face and arms. From his earliest years they irritated him. One day he asked Mother why she soaked clothes in bluing, and she replied, "To bleach them—make them white." The next day Paul Candler was missing so long that a search began. It ended in the bathroom, where he lay soaking himself and his freckles in a tub full of bluing water.

An urge in church was quietly but just as surely expressed. Once Papa announced, "Let us sing hymn number 135. Please stand on the last verse." During the pause just before the last stanza, when the congregation was rising, Candler, who had been sitting next to the aisle, calmly stepped out from his pew, laid his songbook on the floor, and carefully stood on the last verse.

The Sunday before, on Father's Day, Papa found a card on his breakfast plate with a poem on it written by Candler, who called him "Pop." It read:

> In and out, all about,
> You're the poppiest Pop, without a doubt,
> But nobody is dissatisfied.

Mother's favorite story was of the day Paul Candler was born. A neighborly parishioner who had stood by her through the event picked up the tiny, squirming bundle and peered into its beetlike face.

"Just think," she gasped, "this makes nine, and not an idiot in the bunch!"

Remember the Sabbath Day

"WHAT is your formula for successful preaching, Brother Jones?" a member of the white race once asked a renowned black parson.

"Well, sir," came his reply, "I always makes three points. Firstly I tells 'em I'm gonna tell 'em; secondly I tells 'em; and thirdly I tells 'em I've done told 'em!"

That is descriptive of our family's three-point observance of the Sabbath. On Saturday we remembered to remember the Sabbath Day, on Sunday we remembered, and on Monday we remembered that we had remembered.

The most important day of the week is Saturday. If there be those who deny this go mark them well; they have never lived in a parsonage. Since Sunday was the day around which our career in common revolved, it took great preparation to do the day jus-

25

tice. And Saturday was the eve.

From six o'clock in the morning until midnight the day was foreordained to the exclusive pursuit of getting ready for Sunday. Promptly after morning prayer and breakfast Papa went to his study at the church to prepare the sermon for Sunday. Hugh and Cecil set out with broom and dustcloth to shine the church for Sunday. Edd and Janette set in with broom and mop to polish the house for Sunday. Raybon took down the ironing board to press the clothes for Sunday. Gil stayed on duty to answer telephone calls concerning Sunday. Candler and I skimmed over the dishes and bounded outdoors to store up play to tide us over Sunday. And Mother took down the pots and pans to prepare the food for Sunday.

Like Siamese twins the church and parsonage were ever side by side. And as Papa sat in his study concentrating on Sunday's sermon, into his thoughts filtered the buzzing of his swarm of bees—the yodeling of Hugh and Cecil echoing through the emptiness of the church, the rhythmic knocking of a broom handle contacting church pews, the whoops and shouts of our gang playing Indian in the backyard, the robust whistling of Edd as he cleaned the house, the incessant ringing of the telephone, and the aroma of pies and cakes emanating from the kitchen.

It all registered in the study. Proof of it came one Saturday morning when I became incensed at the action of a playmate. Standing beneath Papa's window I unwisely dared to shout, "I'll be John Brown!"

The moment it was out grave doubt assailed me. We were not allowed to give vent to our emotions with violent language. Mother reminded us, "And as he knew not what to say, he swore," and Papa placed a penalty on every step from the path of pure speech. His nearest approach to profanity was a disapproval-laden "Sh-h-h-h!" This he used to convey extreme annoyance, disgust, or denunciation. But this he also used with different intonations and facial expression to show embarrassment, approval, or delight. The barometer of Papa's reaction to any situation lay in the force and tone of his "Sh-h-h-h!"

With "I'll be John Brown" I had put my foot into it. On its heels came a vigorous "Sh-h-h-h!" through the window, and out the door came Papa. He took me by the arm into the house, where Mother washed the flour from her hands and with soap washed the profanity from my mouth. For the next two hours I sat quietly in a chair by Papa feeling that I was a transgressor most unworthy. The "I'll be John Brown" mode of speech was thereafter reserved for days when Papa's Sunday sermon did not station him in the study.

So jealous were Candler and I of Gil's important position as custodian of doorbell and telephone that our Saturday morning play was interspersed with giving false alarms at the front door.

We were especially envious of the telephone conversations. Like every parsonage telephone, ours was afflicted with chronic ringitis, suffering a severe attack each Saturday requiring the constant attention of one person. Gil wore his appointment with a superior air. One day Edd remarked, "Gil, you're a regular bureau of information." That sounded impressive, and Gil lost no opportunity ever after to remind us that he and no other was the "Hero of Information."

One Saturday morning when Mother happened to be in the front of the house entertaining morning callers Gil came in saucer-eyed. "Mother," he said in awe, "come to the back door. On the step is an angel unawares!"

Candler and I crowded past Mother as she walked through the kitchen to see the visitor. It loomed in the doorway, more unaware than angel. The only halo was a fringe of matted hair, and the only robe was a covering of faded, tattered demin. Out of a toothless mouth encompassed by a grizzly beard came an unangelic mumble, "Mornin', kind lady. Could you spare a hungry man a bite to eat?" His nearest approach to the celestial came with the shy radiance which filled his being at sight of the wedge of apple pie and the cup of steaming coffee handed to him by Mother.

"Angel unawares!" we taunted Gil. "That's just another hobo!" But indelibly Gil's Sunday-school teacher had drawn upon his mind the vision of an angel under every bundle of rags.

Hobos seemed to grow on trees in the small towns where we lived, and a slight puff of wind would drop one on our doorstep. The wind was always high on Saturday morning, strangely coincidental with Mother's baking. Being servants of the Lord, we could not deny loaves and fishes to our fellowmen, however multitudinous they might become.

Saturday morning chores were finished and dinner over by one o'clock. The buzz of the morning hours subsided into a low hum as the four older boys left for their jobs of delivering groceries or mowing lawns; as Janette took over the ironing; as Papa left for town to get his hair cut, buy groceries, and mingle with the Saturday crowd; and as Mother sat down with her mending to catechize us younger children on the Sunday-school lesson. If we had already learned it—oh ecstasy! two of us might go with Papa. We would swing patiently one to each of his hands, our short steps trying to keep pace with his long-legged stride.

At the square, while Papa got his haircut, we could sometimes sit with little friends from the country in a wagon hitched in the center of activity. Then we would accompany Papa on his journey around the business quadrangle. Our progress was like the proverbial frog trying to get out of the well, hopping one foot up and falling two feet back, as Papa would take a step and then fall back for conversation.

"How are you, Brother Haskins?" he would say. "And are the children all well? How is your wife?" Adding a few more pleasantries about the crops and the weather we would move on a pace only to be stopped.

"Howdy, Preacher," would come a friendly voice from another direction. We would get all set for another pause. There was nothing to do but stand first on one foot and then on the other, or entertain each other by making funny faces. Papa's invariable hopeful hint, "I'll see you at church in the morning," was the indication that now we could be moving on.

The final stop in town was at the grocery store, where in addition to last-minute supplies for Sunday, Papa bought twenty-five cents' worth of mixed candy.

When at five o'clock he stepped through the door at home he was greeted with whoops of joy and followed to the front bedroom. There he dumped the candy into the middle of the bed, and as we stood around, his voice in doting tone called our names while he distributed the sweets. "This is for you, Janette. Save this for Edd. Here's yours, Gil." And on down the line, showing no partiality, even to the baby. No candy was ever so delicious, and no window display of sweets on any city street has ever held the charm of that front-room bed.

After that everybody, in high mood, helped with supper. It had to be dispensed with in short order. Cleanliness is next to godliness, and eleven o'clock Sunday morning must see the entire family—seven masculine members, and three feminine ones—shining and clean, in best bib and tucker, seated in church.

Before that coat of sheen, however, came the matter of baths, and as the boys grew older, shaves. Papa was firm that there be no baths and no shaves on Sunday. And the Sabbath began exactly on the stroke of midnight.

With the swallowing of the last supper crumb, the

cleansing process began. Baths were taken in order of age, beginning with Candler, the baby, that he might be the first to bed. That left the older boys free to turn the ice-cream freezer—for Sunday's dessert—or to witness weddings. It left Papa free till the last to see that the midnight law was observed, to perform any unexpected wedding, and to polish our shoes.

We wore black shoes, for obvious reasons. Bathroom-bound on Saturday night we detoured by way of the kitchen to leave them. There Papa was settled with a giant bottle of shoe polish and a preoccupied look. Passing through the hall we could hear him accenting the Scripture with a whip of the shine cloth. And by midnight, ready for Sunday, the kitchen floor exhibited a glossy display to make a shoeshop green with envy—"Boots, boots," exactly ten pairs of them.

CAME the Sabbath! The day for which such painstaking preparation had been made. Papa rose at an unearthly hour to go over his sermon, to meditate, and to hide the funny papers. He was a follower of the cartoons, but they did not show their faces before his eyes on the Sabbath. The reading of them was deferred, for himself and for us, until Monday morning—though they were sometimes "accidently" discovered and surreptitiously read.

We were called thirty minutes earlier on Sunday than the usual time for getting up. Instead of the oft-heard phrase "Crawl out," Papa's signal was expressed, "Come crawling." Each morning he went first to the door of the older boys' room. "Hugh, Cecil, Raybon, and Edd," he called in one breath, "come crawling." Then on to our door, "Janette and Alyene," in a slightly modified tone, "come crawling." And to the last bedroom, "Gil and Candler, come crawling."

One Saturday night Cecil suggested to each of us that when Papa delivered his next getting-up call we respond immediately, collectively, and literally. The next morning we were in readiness. "Hugh, Cecil, Raybon, and Edd," Papa began in the usual manner. We lay in the stillness before action until the final note,

"Gil and Candler, come crawling!" Then as if shot from so many guns the eight of us rolled from our beds to the floor and on hands and knees, in pajamas and nightgowns, crawled noisily into the hall and closed in on Papa. He stood in the middle of the clamoring mob. "Sh-h-h-h!" he said with an embarrassed you-got-me-that-time grin. "Mother," he called out, "I wish you'd come look at your children."

AFTER Sunday breakfast Papa distributed the money for our offering. One tenth of his week's salary had been changed into dimes and quarters for that purpose. If the boys were working, it was taken for granted that they would pay their own tithe. Pennies and nickels were never taken to church. They were useful in buying soda pop and chewing gum, but for the Lord they were not enough. When the collection plate glided by with pennies and nickels conspicuous among its treasures, I used to wonder who could have been so callous as to offer such insult to the Lord. But search as I might throughout the congregation, no telltale expression lingered on any face.

While we were dressing for Sunday school one of the boys would be sent to the church to ring the bell. That was for other people. We needed no bell. We had Papa. He went about the house giving time warnings: "Only fifteen minutes till Sunday-school time, children . . . . Mother, it's nearly Sunday-school time," and the final call, "Only five minutes—all out!"

An honest confession is good for the soul: as a child I was not interested in Sunday school. To be sure, when the roll was called each Sunday my body was present, but my mind was still with Alice in Wonderland or whoever might be doing exciting things. It did not occur to me that Sunday school too could be interesting.

Somehow it was my lot to be always in classes taught by elderly women. They were sweet and good, and I respected them. I took it for granted that when one became elderly she would naturally be saintly and would know the Bible cover to cover. For myself it was unnecessary that I think on these things, until the white snows of age should sprinkle my hair; then I too would teach a class of little girls about Moses in the bulrushes. Of course Mother was good and was still young, but then that was different—she was a preacher's wife.

When I was ten, however, and we moved to a city pastorate I had an inner revolution. The first Sunday, when I was shown to the little classroom where sat a dozen girls of my age, I was as usual prepared to think my own thoughts during the lesson period. But here was a picture to make me stop short and leave all prearranged thoughts behind. Seated at the table as one of the class was a young woman of not more than twenty-two. She was gowned in modish dark dress simply accented by a single strand of pearls; her hat was of harmonizing color with the dress; her arms were encased from wrist to elbow in fashionable white kid gloves. And through dark laughing eyes shone a gay spirit. She was vibrant, she was poised—she was beautiful. Could anybody so young and full of the glory of living actually enjoy Sunday school? There was all the evidence. Maybe there was more to all this than I had thought.

For the next three years, my incentive for going to Sunday school was not to swell the attendance, not to learn the Ten Commandments, but to strive toward a pattern which to my little-girl eyes was perfection, and which was ever before me in the person of Kate Tankersley.

EACH Sunday at the eleven o'clock service, as the choir filed in singing, "Holy, holy, holy," Papa seated himself in the pulpit chair and went through an ocular roll call of our pew. Unless some catastrophe prevented, he saw six boys in white starched shirts and creased trousers, two girls with curled hair and ruffled dresses, and Mother looking as fresh and lovely as the flower which unfailingly graced her shoulder.

Mother sat next to the aisle, probably better to establish the eye-to-eye contact with Papa. Throughout the sermon in her own way she would send messages in code to him. A certain glint of the eye meant, "Brush your hair down." Papa would get the hint, and both hands would co-operate in a furtive hair-smoothing. A tilt of Mother's head meant, "You're preaching well; I'm proud of you," and Papa's head would lift two inches, as his words leaped over each other in joyful expression. A straight-from-the-eye gaze warned, "You are preaching too long," at which Papa would close his Bible and make one long slide to the benediction.

After church there was a half hour or so of mingling with friends. During that time Raybon was addicted to going up and down the aisles saying, "Come home with us to dinner." Those he invited invariably accepted, and Mother greeted them as long-expected-and-at-last arrived guests.

Rural members of the church usually saw to it that the festive board at the parsonage yielded up fried chicken on Sunday. But fried chicken without gravy and hot biscuits is like a preacher minus hymnbook and Bible, so Mother properly trimmed the chicken with boats of cream gravy and plates of biscuits. There were always ten of us and from two to six guests at dinner.

When dinner was over we moved into the living room. Skates, bicycles, and games were of no avail on Sunday, but within the pale of permitted pleasures came the making of music. Ragtime melodies were banned. That still left folk music and sentimental popular songs. The family orchestra included, besides

the piano, a xylophone, a violin, a guitar, and eight
strong voices. Everybody performed, individually or
collectively, guests included.

ONE Sunday when the church pianist had stayed with
us and we were comfortably launched on our musical
afternoon, Papa turned to her. "Katie," he asked,
"won't you play for us?"

This particular moment had been anticipated by
Cecil and Raybon earlier in the day. They plotted with
Katie that when Papa's request came she should com-
ply by playing the latest song craze, "Twelfth Street
Rag," calling it by another name. "I'd love to," she
sweetly consented and seated herself at the piano.

"This is a new song," she said, " 'Joy in My
Heart.' " And she began to play. At first she touched
the keys lightly but gradually gathered momentum,
and eventually letting herself go she pounded out
"Twelfth Street Rag" with all the abandon of a night-
club entertainer.

We sat attentively listening, none daring to look at
Papa. Our thoughts were busy imagining what he was
thinking of what passersby were thinking of such
goings-on in the parsonage. When Katie thumped out
the last jazzy notes, there was a pin-dropping pause as
we turned our eyes toward Papa. But there was no
trace of disapproval on his countenance and no "Sh-
h-h-h" upon his lips.

"That's wonderful!" he exclaimed and settled back
into his chair. "Play it again."

Katie repeated her performance, not once but twice.
Through the stillness of Sunday afternoon continued

the pealing forth of "Twelfth Street Rag"—a ragweed which by another name became more sweet.

REMEMBER the Sabbath Day! Our attitude toward its observance was unconsciously expressed by Candler when he was six. One afternoon he was riding with Papa and Mother. "Oh, look at the sheep, Mother!" he exclaimed, pointing across her face.

"Yes, son," she said, gently putting his arm into his lap.

A few minutes later he pointed again. "Look at the windmill, Mother!" he shouted.

"Yes, dear, I see," said Mother, again lowering his arm.

A third time he shot an arm across her face. "Oh, look, Mother!" he cried.

Patience exhausted, she took hold of his arm. "Son," she said firmly, "You *must not* point!"

"Why not, Mother?" he innocently asked. "It's not Sunday, is it?"

We Are Laborers Together With God

WHEN Papa as a minister, with Mother staunchly at his side, joined the crusade for Christianity their enlistment gradually brought to the cause eight young knights of the Holy Grail. As children we felt a grave responsibility in wearing the red plume of helpfulness, in carrying the sword of faith, and in keeping bright the shield of righteousness. We felt wholly capable, as knights, of lowering the drawbridge of the Gospel for sponsoring into the fortress of heaven any seeking one. The very acts of God were accepted as part of our responsibility—sometimes to a painfully literal degree.

On one occasion when the Almighty withheld for a

time a prophesied event, Papa's quartet of knights errant took matters into their own hands.

It was the year of the world's apprehensive waiting for another appearance of Halley's Comet. According to prophecy it would speed toward the earth, brush it with a fiery tail, annihilate all within its path, and then disappear into space for another seventy-six years. Months had passed since scientists first predicted the fearsome event. Each night at dusk the stage was set for nature's greatest performance, and the spectators waited breathlessly. A backdrop of sky, dotted with millions of stars, hung silently waiting; the moon, a giant spotlight, swung into place to illuminate the show; the technicians of heaven spared no effort in creating a perfect setting. Night after night the alfresco audience came to sit and watch, each in his own front yard, and night after night they were disappointed.

Fearful lest some, especially the children, should lose faith in there being a God who could perform such a miracle, Papa's little helpers busied themselves to bring about the appearance of the comet. Leaving their places in the front-yard audience Hugh, Cecil, Raybon, and Edd tiptoed into the house to the closet where Mother kept a bag of rags. Emptying it in haste they carried its contents to the back yard. Cecil paused in the kitchen long enough to stuff his pocket full of matches.

By the light of the moon they found three oversized rocks. These were used for weights. Taking one in his hand Hugh began to wind a cloth tightly around it as the other boys tore strips for more wrapping. Hugh wound and wound. The object grew ever larger until at last it attained what they considered comet propor-

tions. Not forgetting the fiery tail they tied narrow
strips together, attached one end to the comet and
rolled the rest into a ball to be ready for fast unrolling.
For good measure they fashioned two other comets in
identical manner. Laying them on the ground they
brought the kerosene can from the back porch and
saturated the ground around them as well as the comets.

With the necessary properties for the show they cau-
tiously went to their chosen stage—the church. Laden
with the high-smelling comets Hugh and Cecil found
their way through the darkness of the interior and
climbed the rickety ladder to the bell tower. Raybon
and Edd were left aground as spreaders of the alarm.

Cecil, the family's champion rock-thrower, took the
body of the comet into his grip and began to wind up
for throwing it into space. The signal was given to the
boys waiting in the shadows below. Then Hugh struck
a match to ignite the end of the serpentine tail, and on
the split second with great force Cecil hurled the flaming torch into the heavens.

In true Paul Revere style the other boys were already spreading the alarm through the neighborhood.
"Halley's Comet has come! Halley's C-o-m-e-t has
come!" they yelled at a lung-bursting pitch. "Look
toward the church tower—Halley's Comet has come!"

For those who failed to see the first one, the little
lords of creation sent out a second, then a third.

The doorstep audience rose to its feet to stare at the
real, though miniature, streaks of fire falling earth-
ward. Papa straightway left his box seat—the front
porch of the parsonage—and crossed the yard in
double-quick time. Fumbling through the darkness of
the church he too climbed the ladder to the tower, not

to send forth a startling sight but to bring down from their heights two startled creators of comets. At that high point in the show the curtains were drawn. Only the parsonage family from its vantage point backstage was permitted to see the inevitable climax. But it carried a pungent message and the acts of God were left in His own hands—at least for a short time.

A FEW months later Cecil felt compelled to lend assistance again, although this time in a less spectacular manner.

"Vengeance is mine; I will repay, saith the Lord." Cecil lay awake on his bed one night and reminded himself of those words. If he took steps toward a just vengeance, wouldn't he be helping the Lord? With his slingshot he could wreak vengeance on Brother Goodnight. Another thought came all unbidden. Hadn't David helped the Lord by using his sling? Rechristening himself David—and feeling wholly justified—he dressed, jammed his slingshot into his pocket, and slipped quietly out of the house.

The moon was bright, and it was no trouble to find plenty of stones. So armed he made his way to a tree across the road from Brother Goodnight's wagon yard.

The wagon yard was the forefather of the modern tourist camp. Persons traveling the highway could pull their wagons into Brother Goodnight's yard and for the sum of twenty-five cents have a secure night's rest. For summoning him at any hour of the night, a large gong, with a string attached, hung on the gatepost.

Earlier on this particular summer evening, Brother Goodnight had been waiting at the parsonage when Papa came in late from his pastoral calls. As Papa went into the living room he called to Cecil, "Son, go un-harness the horse."

Cecil immediately obeyed, stopping long enough in the lot to pet old Henry. Papa must have driven him long and hard. Perspiration and the pressure of the harness left marks on his body so vivid, that in the moonlight they looked like the harness itself.

The consultation over and Brother Goodnight on his way home, the family sat down to a belated supper, only to be interrupted by a step on the front porch. It was a postscript to Brother Goodnight's visit. His voice came from the darkness. "Preacher, didn't you tell your boy to unharness that horse? Well, I just passed by the lot, and the horse wasn't unharnessed."

Without a word Papa got up from the table and indi-cated by a jerk of the head that he wished to see Cecil on the back porch. There he meted out punishment to fit the crime of disobedience. Cecil made no protest, since he did not dare question the veracity of one of Papa's stewards, and the matter was not mentioned again. But the injustice of it had rankled in his heart all evening, and now he was retaliating.

He climbed the tree opposite the wagon yard, got all set, loaded his slingshot, and with David's true aim sent a rock toward the gong on the gatepost. The bell resounded with all the urgency of a tired customer's string pulling. Obligingly soon, Brother Goodnight popped out the front door in a white nightshirt, split on the sides, and barefoot. He picked his steps carefully through the yard, mumbling sleepily, "Just a minute," and opened the gate. But no wagon appeared, and no wagon driver. He scratched his head, mumbled some-thing else, and found his way back into the house.

Cecil sat patiently in the tree. Before long he took aim with another rock. Again the bell clamored through the stillness of the night, and again in response out popped Brother Goodnight, still barefoot, and still sleepily eager to collect twenty-five cents. But "naught there was stirring in the still, dark night." He was visibly affected but went back to his bed.

Still in his tree Cecil sat, and soon he again sent his missile through the air. This time it was longer before the figure in white padded to the gate. He had probably been mulling over the story of the boy and the wolf but had decided that this time it might really be the wolf—with twenty-five cents between his teeth. When he opened the gate only the crickets' chirping gave sound of life in the night.

Brother Goodnight wearily dragged himself back to his bed to get much-needed sleep. Presently Cecil sent his final shot. He could have held out till dawn, but with the last false alarm, Brother Goodnight's

emotional state hinted of insanity. Cecil knew that re-
venge was finally his and the Lord's, and for himself he
found it delectably sweet.

NOT always were we self-appointed in donning our
knightly armor. Frequently it was thrust upon us, as in
Sister's case.

One day during a study period in school her concen-
tration on arithmetic was broken. "Janette! Janette!"
came a whisper from across the aisle two seats up,
where Vernelle Bates was hunching behind her geography book. "Oh, Janette," she said miserably, "I've
just had the evilest thought! You're a preacher's
daughter, tell me what to do with it," bouncing up
and down in her seat, "tell me what to do with it—
quick!"

"Well," said Sister in guarded whisper, "Just think
of flowers, and—music, and—and—JESUS!" The joy
of having found just the right word for putting Satan
behind brought Sister's tone far above a whisper. The
class was shocked to hear the preacher's daughter
suddenly say "Jesus" aloud. *Ohs* and *ahs* filled the
room.

"Janette," the teacher scolded, "You may stand in
the corner with your face to the wall for the next
hour."

Thus Sister paid the martyr's price and was stoned
with hard looks, all for wearing the red plume of helpfulness.

"MAN'S extremity is God's opportunity." It was
slightly confusing at times to decide in our young
minds just where our responsibility for others ended

and where the Lord's opportunity began. That was in the more subtle spiritual areas of living, however. In the physical realm there was the comforting certainty that no mistake could ever be made in feeding, clothing, or sheltering a human body in distress.

Not only was open house held three hundred and sixty-five days and nights of every year for this purpose, but even the parsonage storm celler was dug larger than average to accommodate the varying needs of the parsonage family, and also to shelter neighbors and transients. Many homes were equipped with storm cellers—" 'fraid holes" we called them—but others were not; therefore ours protected those who had no storm house of their own.

When we moved to West Texas the area had known terrific tornadoes—those swirling, swishing, funnel-shaped clouds which would swoop suddenly to earth and smash everything in their path. Spring of the year was open season for such visitors. Shortly before we were sent to one town, it had been practically blown away. Only a few scattered buildings were left, like blades of grass which have escaped the scythe.

"It sure is hard on us," a steward said jestingly to Papa the day of our arrival, "havin' a cyclone one year and a preacher with eight kids the next."

Our first vision of the new home was of a lonely little house standing forlornly, like a few others, with blinded eyes amid the ruins of less fortunate companion dwellings. All year we burned firewood from the wreckage, and all year we, with the rest of the population, rushed to the storm celler every time the wind began to blow. It was exciting, although frightening, to be torn from slumber and rushed to shelter; for a tornado came quickly and, like the thief, invariably in the night.

Our first knowledge of the impending danger would be a brisk shaking, "Storm is coming, children. We're going to the cellar." There was no time to waste; already the wind would be lashing the trees with a menacing hint of what was to come. Robes must be got into quickly, a pillow and quilt grabbed from the bed, and shoes snatched up. Barefoot we dashed through the kitchen and out the back door by the light of Papa's lantern. There was no time for words as we ducked our heads to brave the wind and scampered the few yards to the storm-house door.

There were usually others in the shelter ahead of us, neighbors with their children, drummers from the local hotel, or whoever might have been caught in the storm. One night when we arrived, ten strong, at the cellar, eighteen people were already huddling in its protecting depths.

About the size of a small room, seven feet underground, the cellar was safe and comfortable. It was floored, ceiled, and covered with heavy timber. On the outside the framework was covered by a mound of dirt built up in a cone, with a pipe through the center for ventilation. At one end was the door, equipped with heavy iron hinges and fitting snugly against the framework of the flat roof. A strong iron clasp on the inside held it securely against the determined wind. Directly under the door were the steps leading down to safety.

On one side of the celler and at one end shelves were built from floor to ceiling for storing the year's supply of preserves, jellies, pickles, and sundry other home-canned food. On the opposite wall hung a lantern. Like the lamps of the five wise virgins, it was kept filled with oil and ever in readiness for burning. Against that wall, running its length, was a low bench where sat the elders during the storm, relating the horrors of other storms, while the children, on a pallet at their feet, listened with wide eyes and receptive ears. It is thrilling to hear of danger when we feel perfectly secure.

Our favorite spinner of yarns was Aunt Mollie Cadwallader. We knew her story from memory, and any child in the neighborhood could have told it word for word—but not with the same emotional fire with which Aunt Mollie related it. As soon as the door was fastened and everybody comfortably seated or sprawled, one of us would pipe up, "Aunt Mollie, tell us about when the cyclone blew you over the windmill."

Aunt Mollie's breath would come faster, her brown eyes would glisten, her ruddy face flush with remembered excitement, as she drew her plump self to the edge of the bench to picture the one dramatic moment of her otherwise uneventful life—the time when, on her way to the storm house, she had felt herself lifted by an overpowering wind to sail through the air over the windmill in company with chickens, chairs, kitchen stove, and washtub, all being hurled pell-mell at dizzy heights. In keeping with the unpredictable antics of a tornado the wind finally lowered her into a cornfield unharmed. In spite of her fright she lived to tell the tale—on any and every occasion.

OFTEN in the midst of a storm would come a banging on the cellar door and desperate shouts, "Let me in! Let me in!" The clasp would be unfastened and the

door pushed up to welcome into the fold some
frightened being, after which it would take a great
struggle against the force of the wind to pull the door
back into place.

The most welcome shout of "Let me in" which ever
came to our ears was heard the night Papa was out in
the storm. He had preached that evening at a church in
the country and had not returned when Mother roused
us from sleep. "We're going to the cellar," she said.

"Where's Papa, Mother? Where's Papa?" we cried
as we scrambled in semidarkness to the back door,
where Mother stood in Papa's usual place holding the
lantern.

"Your father hasn't come from Centerville," she
said quietly. "He'll find a storm house on his way."
But in the light of the lamp her face was pale, and
behind the outward calm of her voice there was a note
of anxiety. Carrying Candler she followed us into the
shelter.

"Don't fasten the door yet," she said to a neighbor
as he closed the opening. "There may be others coming."

But the storm grew worse, and for the safety of
those inside the door was fastened. Mother sat on the
bench near the door.

"This is going to be a real twister," said one of the
men. "Lots of wind in that cloud." Mother raised her
eyes anxiously to his face but said nothing.

The usual tales were told, with corresponding comment, but we had no ear for tales that night. For Papa
was not there. Had he found shelter? Was he still in the
church? On the road? Where was he?

"I reckon he wouldn't try to make it when he saw

the storm gathering,'' said another neighbor in an attempt to be comforting. The cellar, usually so cheerful, so safe and secure, seemed tonight musty and dim and lonely.

After what seemed an eternity there was a sudden pounding on the door, and Papa's voice, sounding strangely far away, shouted, ''Open the door! Open the door!''

Before any of the men could get to it Mother was unfastening the clasp; and Papa, dripping but thankful, came out of the storm. His story took precedence, as he told how the storm had overtaken him while he rode along in his buggy, searching between flashes of lightning for the sight of a farmhouse. None came to view. He could not see to guide old Henry and was forced to slack the rein completely, giving the horse his head with the hope that the animal would bring him safely home. The flashes of lightning, which did not reveal a haven, disclosed a black cloud hovering nearer as old Henry, sensing the danger, strained to outdistance the ominous storm.

''The cloud was right on my heels when I came in,'' Papa said. ''I'm sure it will strike near the town if not in it.'' We could visualize our home being blown to splinters.

The next day dawned serene and clear, however, with few evidences that the elements had so recently been on a rampage. But as Papa looked out toward his church he saw on the vacant lot next to it evidence of one of nature's whimsical jokes. A vestibule, bearing all the earmarks of the Baptist church, and looking the worse for a night out, was brazenly leaning for support on the Methodist church.

WHEN we were moved from the West Texas town to a
city church in North Texas we had a tornado hang-
over. As we had no storm house, whenever a threatening cloud arose it prompted the family to streak out the
back door with complete regalia into the church basement for shelter.

City life was different in other ways. No longer did
Papa drive old Henry. Now he owned a car—a shining
model T Ford sedan which we called the "Gospel
Chariot." For although our surroundings were different, our responsibility for the welfare of others remained unchanged, and the wheels of the family car
turned incessantly on business for the church. It called
for and delivered to the church door any member who
could not get there for reasons of lameness, age, or
distance. It delivered groceries from the church to the
poor. It carried Papa to weddings, funerals, and sick-
rooms. But not always was Papa at the wheel. Often it
was one of the boys. Raybon or Edd would help
Grandmother Lacy down the steps of the church teasing and flattering her as he went, help her into the car,
and take her home, while his date for the evening
waited at the parsonage until he could come back to
the church to get Brother Crutcher, whose foot was
injured. When all the dependent ones were tucked
away safely, each in his own front door, then he
might abandon himself to carefree times with his
friends.

"But Papa," Edd was heard to protest one evening,
"I've had this date for over a week."

"I'm sorry, son." Papa was firm. "The business of
the church comes first. You'll have to bring Mrs. Clark
and Mrs. Farrell to the service. I'm sure Mary won't

mind." And Edd accepted the command without
further comment.

Although driving the "Gospel Chariot" was assigned only to the boys, Sister and I also had our place
in working with Papa. We visited and read to the shut-
ins. We were not allowed to go where there might be
contagious disease, but for the aged and invalids there
was also need of cheer. Inconsistent with his care for
our safety, Papa never hesitated to go where illness
might be, however contagious its nature. He believed
that as long as he was doing his work no ill would befall
him. He spent hours among the sick without once con-
tracting a contagious disease or bringing the germ
home to his family. The conviction that his work was
dear to God and could not be spared was always his
bulwark.

ONE of Papa's favorite tasks in his work as a crusader
was the promotion of interracial understanding. At
every available opportunity his pulpit was filled by a
missionary on furlough or by a member of another
race.

One Sunday evening the sermon hour was given
over to a Japanese lecturer. Papa had spread the news,
and the familiar faces of the congregation were flanked
by the unfamiliar countenances of visitors. As the se-
date little man of the yellow race took his place behind
the pulpit after him tagged his small son, a dark-
skinned lad with slanting eyes, shiny ebony hair, and a
button nose. During his father's lecture he stood
quietly by his side, not a disturbing factor, but an in-
triguing addition to the picture—especially for the
children of the congregation.

Candler, whose usual demeanor in church was on

the fidgety side, sat noticeably still, fascinated by the sight of a Japanese boy just his size. During the first part of the lecture he did not take his eyes from his brother-under-the-skin. Mother, sitting by him, was unaware of the wool his mind was gathering. The inspired lecturer held his audience enthralled, while relating his conversion to Christianity in a remote mission in Japan.

"I went to the missionary after the service," he said in broken English, "and I told him, 'I must know this Christ of whom you speak.' "

Unnoticed Candler slid from his seat and was soon standing on the rostrum by the little visitor. As the lecture went on Candler peered intently into the face of the other child. A passive smile flitting across it was the only response. Candler then walked around back of him and looked as intently from the other side. By this time there were faint giggles among the children of the audience. Oblivious of everything and everybody but himself and the object of his scrutiny, Candler returned to the first side. After a swift renewal of that view he grabbed the button nose of the Japanese lad and pulled it to the limit of his strength.

Japanese epithets and small fits immediately filled the air, until Papa shamefacedly disentangled the two and offered apologies to father and son. The lecture was resumed, but any discussion of better understanding between the white race and the yellow seemed futile after the exhibition of interracial harmony which had just taken place.

ON another occasion a missionary recently returned from China was filling the pulpit. For the sake of the younger children who had not yet learned it in school, he reminded the listeners that China is opposite us on the globe, so that if we bored a hole through the earth we should come out in China.

What child has not pondered this long and wonderingly? And which of the realists among them has not started digging in the earth with the intention of finding out for himself if it is actually true? Unless it be those like us, who though curious were also cautious, since somehow within our childish minds had lodged the belief that the bottomless pit of hell was in the earth beneath us. One day Gil, Candler, and I debated long as to whether to dig a tunnel to China, but decided against it lest we inadvertently unearth one of Satan's imps—or even Satan himself.

A reminder of the geographical location of China by the lecturer sent Gil's thoughts again going over the problem, and when the speaker in conclusion said, "Are there questions any of you would like to ask?" Gil, ever the seeker of information, rose importantly to the height of his nine years.

"Please, sir," he said, with a wrinkle of seriousness in his forehead, "I'd like to ask a question. Did you have to go through hell to get to China?"

FROM the time she was thirteen, Sister was commissioned by Papa to take up the shield of righteousness every Sunday afternoon and superintend the Junior Epworth League, attended by children between the ages of five and twelve. She played the piano for the singing of hymns, read the Scriptures, and taught the younger ones how to be Christian soldiers. Following Papa's precepts, she stressed the need of understanding those of other races.

One spring near the Easter season, after a fervent speech from Sister, Candler became imbued with missionary zeal, and wanted to take immediate action.

"I think the Lord would be happy," he said, "if we had an Easter egg hunt for the Mexican children."

The spirit of giving ran like wildfire over the juvenile assemblage. We crowded around Sister. "Oh, let's do!" we begged. "Please, let's do."

And although Sister knew that she would be in the midst of examinations at the university the week of Easter, she consented.

The next day an invitation was sent to the City Mexican Mission, to seventy-five children. It was happily accepted. A park was chosen for the hunt, and the time and place were announced. An entire week was spent by the children of the Epworth League and their mothers boiling eggs, dying them, and imprinting fancy designs over the dye—pictures of rabbits, of flowers, of comic faces, and of nothing in particular. Six hundred eggs were prepared for one hundred children—seventy-five brown-skinned guests, and twenty-five Junior League hosts.

Came the day, and at long last three o'clock in the afternoon. Cars driven by missionary-minded parents of our members transported the guests from mission to park. And on the designated spot one hundred children gathered, each with gift basket on his arm, eagerly awaiting the signal for the hunt to begin.

Sister pulled a policeman's whistle from her pocket, and at its shrill cry, children scattered in all directions like a swarm of bees set free in a flower garden. Bending near a bush or shrub momentarily, they would swoop up an egg, dispose of it, then fly to another.

Strolling here and there among the celebrators Sister took in the strange fact that only American children had eggs in their baskets. Thinking she would be of help she fell in step with a Mexican boy. His quick eye ferreted out the nearest egg before she could show it to him, and she stood aghast as he paused, not to drop it into the basket, but to stuff it with both hands into his mouth—pictures, dye, shell, and all. In less time that it takes to tell it went the way of all food, and he was off to find another. Sister looked about her in alarm to see countless other little Mexicans devouring their eggs in like manner. It had not occurred to anyone that these children might not be familiar with our custom of having Easter-egg hunts.

Sister stood petrified. The dye was poisonous she was sure. Across her mind moved the vision of a long procession and a mass funeral in Little Mexico on the morrow. She set about trying to save this one and that one, but they persisted in stuffing eggs down their throats. Sister stood helplessly by as one lad consumed five, six, seven, eight eggs.

"Candler," she yelled at the top of her voice. Candler rushed to her side.

"Make him stop eating those eggs," she pleaded. "He's killing himself."

Candler remonstrated with the boy. "Don't eat those," he said. "You'll be sick."

Since of the object of concern could not understand English, he went blissfully on his dangerous way, devouring each egg as he found it. Candler's red hair bristled at being thus ignored in an attempt to save a life. He abandoned all efforts at speech and resorted to the common language of fists. He rushed at the lad, snatching a half-eaten egg from him.

"Boy, look—a fight!" someone yelled. In the next few seconds the pals of each boy were rushing to his defense. Then the pals of the pals rushed to their defense, and the missionary enterprise ended in a free-for-all between American hosts and Mexican guests.

At home Sister buried her head on Mother's shoulder.

"I've killed them," she sobbed. "They'll every one be dead tomorrow—from poisoning."

Mother went to the telephone. "Doctor Baird," she said to our family physician, "Janette's Junior League entertained some Mexican children with an Easter-egg hunt, and they ate eggshells and all. Do you think the dye or the shell could kill them?"

A loud laugh rang through the telephone into the room. "Kill them?" he roared. "If they can eat chili and tamales, a little dye and eggshell won't hurt 'em."

Pray Without Ceasing

PAPA'S contemporaries in the ministry have often marveled that it was possible on a preacher's income to clothe, feed, and give college educations to eight children.

The amount of a Methodist clergyman's salary is common knowledge. The church members know it, as they determine the sum and pay it. Other ministers and congregations know it, as the published minutes of the Conference each year record every pastor's salary—the amount assessed and the amount paid. Therefore it is also common knowledge that "he is rich only from the very want of wealth."

One day the wife of a neighboring pastor said, "Brother Porter, my husband and I have only three children, and it's nip and tuck to get by. Our income is about the same as yours; how do you and Mrs. Porter manage with eight?"

"Well, Sister Preston," Papa replied, a smile playing over his face, "we eat lots of beans and cornbread."

The Puritans had a common saying that brown bread and the gospel is good fare. We fared well on beans, cornbread, and the gospel. But there were other factors. "More things are wrought by prayer than this world dreams of." When the web of any one life, or of our family life, became a tangled skein, Mother, who talked little with people, talked much with God. After which invariably (and often miraculously) the knots loosened to create an opening, not always where it was expected, but frequently leading to a happier way.

Papa prayed too—without ceasing. He prayed for his flock—for the health of the sick, for the souls of the lost, for the heartening of the discouraged. He prayed early, he prayed late. Each morning at breakfast he read from the Scriptures and offered a prayer. Just before going to bed we knelt in a family group while Mother, or one of us, led the worship. We took turn about, beginning with Hugh, the oldest, and going down the line. "Whose night is it for prayers?" Papa asked nightly. "I did last night," one would speak up. Whereupon Papa would hand the Bible to the one next in years.

WE were trained to pray aloud not only at the table and at the family altar but also in church. Although I took joy in being a little Christian soldier, to me that part of it was hard—praying aloud. Not that I did not want to pray, or felt any hesitancy in approaching God, but He was such a real Personality that I could not bring myself to be confidential with Him in the presence of others. How could a child say, with everybody listening, "Dear God, forgive me; I told a story today"? Other people did not need to know.

And in a family circle of fourteen other juvenile ears, twelve of them attached to the mischievous minds of boys, anything I might say in confidence to God could later be twisted and used against me—as it once was against Gil. One night he opened his heart to God as in a fervent boyish prayer ending with, "And help me to be a good boy. Amen"; and we rose from our knees to go to bed.

"Mother," said Candler, breaking the hush of reverence that had lingered, "I think it's just plain silly. Every time Gil prays he says, 'Lord, help me to be a good boy,' and he never does a thing to help himself!"

To guarantee escape from such embarrassment I squirmed out of my night to lead prayer whenever possible. I pretended to be too sleepy, and Mother would fill in for me. Then I would rush to our room ahead of Sister to fall on my knees by the bed, fully awake.

"O God," an apology would tumble out, "forgive me for not talking to You before the others." And with a feeling of perfect understanding my heart's sincere desire would then be uttered.

But escape from prayer at the table or at church was not so easily managed. Words for these, however, I could usually learn from the others and repeat in impressive tone. If people were to hear a prayer, it must be eloquent; for God my own simple words were adequate.

At the table Cecil once said, "Father, we humbly thank Thee for Thy blessings. Forgive us our trespasses. For Christ's sake. Amen."

That sounded perfect to me. It could be used both as a table blessing and as a sentence prayer at church. I tucked it away in my memory and for several months brought it to my lips in every emergency. But not without brotherly protest.

"Papa," Gil scornfully said, "Alyene doesn't pray. She just turns her mind off and repeats what she has heard somebody else say!"

"Anyway," I said in self-defense, "I do know the meaning of the words I say."

That was rubbing salt on one of Gil's old wounds. When he was very young, still in the Now-I-lay-me-down-to-sleep stage of praying, a farmer gave him a rooster for a pet. He promptly named it "Fie-shi-die."

"Mother, have you some scraps for Fie-shi-die?" he would say, or, "Listen to Fie-shi-die crow!"

"Where on earth did you get such a name?" Edd asked. "Fie-shi-die!"

"Oh, you know," Gil importantly replied, "a rooster crows before you wake—'Fie-shi-die before I wake, I pray the Lord my soul to take.' "

At Wednesday-night prayer meeting, it was expected that every person present should offer a short prayer. My reticence in praying aloud was evidently shared by many people; there were fewer at that service than at any other. We always went, school lessons or not, and Papa could be certain of nine persons at the service.

Without his knowing it, we had an understanding among ourselves that no two of us should ever enter the church together on prayer-meeting night. That was because it was such fun to watch Papa's reactions. During the ten minutes before the service we filtered in, one at a time. Each time a step was heard in the vestibule Papa's face would light up. Which faithful member would it be, thought he, coming out tonight through the rain? His eyes would be riveted to the door in expectancy as the knob would turn, as the door would open, and as through the passage would step, not a faithful member, but another one of his children, whom he knew would be there anyhow. His face would visibly fall. Eight times before every prayer meeting it happened, and every time Papa's face took on an elevatorish aspect as it soared up, only to drop down.

In one town, besides Mother and the eight of us, Papa could count on another regular attendant—prayer-minded Brother Jasper. Every Wednesday night he came, rain or hail, sleet or snow, to sit in the

same corner of the same pew and to pray the same
prayer. It was for his two sons, who never darkened a
church door, but spent their days in riotous living—
playing Bunko and Forty-two. When the time came for
prayer and Papa said, "Let us pray. Won't each of you
offer a sentence prayer?" Brother Jasper was, without
fail, the first to respond.

"O Lord," his regular petition came, "My boys are
out playing *Broncho* and *Forty-four*—have mercy on
their souls!" Whereupon he would immediately fall
asleep and leave everything in the hands of the Lord.

After each member of the family had voiced suppli-
cations in prayer meeting, we came home and as usual
had family prayer. The praying position became as
natural as standing or sitting. This was borne out one
Sunday night. We had been home from church an hour
and were gathering for family worship. Mother looked
over the assemblage.

"Father," she said with great concern, "there's one
missing!"

Prayers were suspended while Papa went back to
the church. He found Gilderoy between the first and
second pews, just as he had knelt for the benediction,
sound asleep!

THE habit of prayer took deep root in our childhood,
but with the forming of the habit there were a few slips.

One Sunday afternoon, as we started out to Junior
Epworth League, Papa was detained by the arrival of a
couple who wished to be married. The boys had gone
to the church ahead, and Papa sent Sister and me on to
begin the service, while he attended to the nuptials.
Since Sister was ten, and I six, by right of seniority she

took charge. We sang "When the Roll Is Called Up Yonder" as lustily as would any fifteen unrestrained children.

"Now let us pray," said Sister with solemn devoutness. "Will every one of you offer a sentence prayer. Just say to Jesus exactly what is in your heart."

As Papa stepped into the vestibule, thirty pious little knees were bended in prayer, and childish voices were raising petitions to heaven. He waited for a more timely entrance.

That very week Sister had made a conquest of the town's most eligible ten-year-old and was claiming him for a sweetheart—to the heartbreak of Plassette Brown. Plassette was the first to respond with just what was in her heart.

"Dear Jesus," she begged, "make that preacher's daughter quit stealing my sweetheart—and send him back to me."

There was a weighty pause. From where Papa was

standing in the doorway he could see that Edd was
kneeling in the opposite direction to his pew, holding
hands under it with Sarah Gross, who was kneeling in
the row behind. Sarah was inspired by Plassette's
frank plea to God.

"Please, dear heavenly Father," she put in her plea,
as her hand tightened on Edd's. "You know I need a
husband—give me Edd Porter for my own."

And, still waiting for an entrance, Papa next recog-
nized the piping voice of the daughter of his leading
steward.

"Dear God," she said, "do keep Mama and Papa
from fussing so much of the time."

DURING revival meetings each summer the afternoons
were devoted to prayer meetings. The men met in the
business section, the women in homes, and the children at the church. One summer we met with Miss
Paddy, an elderly, hard-of-hearing music teacher, as
leader to pray for the sinners of the community. The
devotional service was always the same. One of us
chose a hymn, all of us sang it, then we knelt in
prayer—Miss Paddy at the piano stool, and we at our
pews, in as many different positions as there were
children.

For two days we managed. But the third day began
to tax even our imaginative minds. After some ten of
us had said in the same or similar words, "God bless
all the sinners and make them repent," we were at our
wit's end. On the fourth day, however, little Lizzie
White came bearing a lifesaver, a small book of
prayers. Promptly after the unison kneeling she took it
from her pocket, read a prayer, and passed it down the

line. With renewed interest in the prayer meetings we
read the beautiful ready-made petitions—and sailed
through the remaining days of that revival on flowery
beds of ease.

One prayer became my favorite, and I read it several
days in succession. It lodged in my memory as one to
use when the occasion arose for praying aloud. The
following week when it fell my night for leading family
worship, there was no evasion. I was wide awake and
gladly took up the Bible, as Papa handed it to me. I
read, "The Lord is my shepherd; I shall not
want . . . ." And we knelt together for prayer.

"Hail, Mary, full of grace," I began in dramatic
whisper, "the Lord is with thee." Then proudly,
"Blessed art thou among women . . . . Holy Mary,
Mother of God, pray for us sinners . . . ."

Papa was suddenly seized with a fit of coughing, and
Mother did not restrain her laughter.

EVEN Papa himself has made slips in prayer. One evening as he went out the door to prayer meeting Mother
said, "Don't forget, Father, if Mrs. Gingle is there, ask
her if we can borrow her washpot tomorrow."

Papa was unusually tired, and when during sentence
prayers Brother Sankey went into a list of endless in-
structions to God, Papa must have dozed. The drone
of Brother Sankey's voice suddenly stopped, and Papa
roused with the startled realization that he must close
the prayers. His subconscious mind was still in con-
trol.

"Our heavenly Father," he began sanctimoniously,
"bless the washpot . . . ."

He has never lived it down.

One morning Papa was entertaining an infant grand-daughter before breakfast. We heard them in the living room.

"Who is Grandfather's pal?"

"Carolyn is."

"That's right!" he said. "Now throw the ball to Grandfather. That's a smart girl. Now walk for Grandfather. That's a big girl." And as he heard the breakfast call, "Breakfast is ready; let Grandfather carry you to the table."

Papa does not make transitions rapidly. Seated at the table as we bowed our heads he began the blessing, "Our Grandfather in heaven, we thank Thee . . . ."

Nor will he ever live that down.

Renew a Right Spirit
Within Me

AS SUNDAY eclipsed all other days of the week for us, so two seasons of the year dwarfed others into comparative obscurity—Conference time in October and revival time in the summer. Summer is revival time by virtue of off-season for business, farming, and school, thereby giving ample time for continuous churchgoing.

New members come to the church of today through the avenue of church-school training. But in our childhood it was the old-time religion, vigorously voiced from the pulpit, which brought sinners to the altar and

saw them soundly converted. Many Christian leaders
of today date their usefulness in life from the hour of
conversion in a revival meeting. Members were received in bundles at the closing services of revival
meetings. That was harvest time for the church. The
seeds were planted throughout the year, the grain was
cut during two weeks of services—tender stalks and
tougher ones—and on the last night the sheaves were
gathered and garnered.

All of Papa's work was glorious to him, but his
greatest exhilaration came with "bringing in the
sheaves." His zeal and complete joy in leading souls to
the Kingdom is visible in a written record which he
now cherishes containing the name of every convert in
all his revivals.

WE usually remember best what has caused us the
greatest embarrassment, and one convert in particular
stands out in Papa's memory.

One evening he was jogging along in his buggy on a
country road toward a village where he had been engaged to hold a revival meeting. He had never been to
the community before and knew no one in it. However, he had explicit directions to the home of Dan
Holden, where he was to stay. Papa had intended to
arrive sooner but was delayed, and now realizing that
it was growing dark, he slapped the reins against old
Henry's back. But no sooner had the horse quickened
his pace than Papa tugged at the reins, bringing him to
an abrupt halt. In the dim half light of dusk Papa saw a
man stumbling heavily along the road. He tied the lines
and leaped out of the buggy.

"Here, let me help you," he said as he placed a
supporting arm about the man.'

"Sure," heaved a foggy voice. "I wuzh isht about t'

fall, wuzhn't I, par'ner?'' And across Papa's nostrils was wafted the heavy aroma of corn liquor.

Feeling now that he was aiding not only a needy body, but also a sick soul, Papa helped him into the buggy.

"I'll take you where you are going," he said.

"Ha, ha, wuzhn't goin' a shingle place, par'ner," the vagabond declared, slapping his knee in delight at the joke he had on Papa.

"Then I'll take you home," Papa said.

"Nope," he mumbled. "Lef' home a long time ago, an' I cain't go back." He tugged at his hip pocket and with great effort succeeded in pulling from it a half-empty bottle. "You're a g-good shoak," he went on, and thrust the bottle uncertainly at Papa. "Here, 'ave a d-drink."

Papa diverted the conversation and pondered where to land his strange cargo. He could not get the consent of his inner self to let the man out of the buggy to continue on his downward way. Yet he knew no one in town. "I'll ask the Holdens to keep him overnight," he decided, "and if they don't have room for more than one guest I'll sleep on a pallet."

He stopped the buggy in front of the house, and the Holdens came down the path to meet him. "I have a friend with me," Papa explained. "This is Mr. Lane, Mrs. Holden—and Mr. Holden. I wonder if you could lodge him overnight?"

"Sure, sure," Mr. Holden said cordially. "Any friend of the preacher's is welcome here. Now you jest get out an' go in with my wife, Mr. Lane, an' I'll go around to the barn with Brother Porter an' unhitch his horse."

While the horse was being made comfortable in the barn, the inebriated knight of the road was making himself comfortable in the parlor. Propping his feet high on a table, he became confidential with Mrs. Holden and her mother, who were solicitously hovering over their guest.

"Ye know," he told them with a wink tinged with satisfaction, "me an' the preacher 've been havin' a time!" He pulled out the bottle, fondled it, and continued. "He took a shwig, an' I took a shwig. Ever' time I took a shwig, he took a shwig. Me an' the preacher 're par'nersh."

Circumstantial evidence is a mighty force. But Papa braved it and conducted a successful revival. Among the converts was the devil's disciple himself, who became so attached to Papa that he sobered up and stayed around to hear the preaching. The third night of the meeting he rose from the mourners' bench.

"I'm goin' home," he shouted in great exultation. And with that he walked out.

For years I wondered why Papa so often preached from the text, "Let there be light." Mother offered this explanation: During the first years of his ministry Papa often held camp meetings. Upon a fixed date, families for miles around would come in wagons to meet in a grove and set up camp. They would bring bedsprings, mattresses, cooking utensils, and food. In the center of the grove was a brush arbor where services were held morning, afternoon, and night. For three weeks the community on wheels would sleep, cook, eat, and praise God in the open air.

Light for evening worship was provided by gasoline lanterns hung at uncertain intervals throughout the arbor.

Kneeling on the hay at the altar in such a dimly lit arbor one night was a young man. Night after night he had come to the mourners' bench to grapple with his obdurate self. It has been said that men wish to be saved from the mischief of their vices, but not from their vices. It was evident, however, that this penitent was sincere in his determination to reform, but as his sins were numerous his plight was unyielding. Kneeling closely about him, praying earnestly, were a number of church members and Papa. They prayed, and the choir softly sang. But he made no move. Again they prayed and as the choir began,

> If you are tired of the load of your sin
> Let Jesus come into your heart,

there came the sound of hurrying footsteps from the rear of the arbor. A burly young man rushed toward the contrite one. It was his best friend, who had been converted the night before. He pushed his way through the group and placed two large, rough hands on a bowed head. Shaking it forcefully he asked with fellow feeling, "What's the matter, old boy? Can't you come through?" And then with a helpful mauling he insisted, "Come on through, old fellow—come on through!"

Papa bore the discomfort as long as he could; then he whispered, "I'm sorry, son, but you've got the wrong head!"

"THE old order changeth, yielding place to new." Brush arbors with gasoline lanterns gave way to wooden tabernacles with electric lights, and as churches were built the revivals were often held indoors, despite the heat. But the brighter lights illumined the same dramatic proceedings—and attracted the same June bugs, candle flies, moths, and other insects that infect a Texas night. I can well believe the scholars who claim Beelzebub means "Prince

of Flies,'' for usually the revival was a pitched battle,
with the evangelist and his Gospel fighting the combined forces of sin and the bugs. It took grit and grace
to elevate the minds of the assemblage above these
devilish onslaughts, but the evangelist was invariably
victorious.

Every summer Papa spent weeks away from home
holding revivals for other pastors, but he seldom conducted his own. For them he would secure a professional team—an evangelist and a gospel singer. This
was purposely planned so that the highly accented two
weeks might contrast with the Sunday-to-Sunday worship. Papa began months ahead, dispatching letters far
and wide to procure the best team available. Famous
combinations—an evangelist with fire and a singer
with persuasive tones—were much in demand and had
to be booked long in advance.

As the actual time drew near, Papa moved at concert
pitch. He saw that the pews got a new coat of varnish.
He assigned the women of the church their respective
days for entertaining preachers. He commissioned the
boys to nail placards in bold type, shouting the news,
on every telephone pole in town. He cajoled one of the
merchants into donating scores of palm-leaf fans. He
announced the meeting at rhythmic intervals in each
service and ended every conversation with, ''Our revival begins two weeks from Sunday,'' or, ''Only one
more week until our revival.''

The whole community became abuzz with talk of the
revival. Women cleaned house, baked pies and cakes,
and discussed over the fence their menus for the day
the preachers would dine with them. Mother had to be
reached through a cloud of dust emanating from gen-
eral house cleaning, for the evangelist customarily

stayed at the parsonage. Men in the community worked overtime that they might be at leisure later, for there were morning services and afternoon prayer meetings as well as night services. Nobody planned to go away. Instead relatives were invited to "come on" for visits and attend the revival. Lovers sighed in sheer ecstasy over the prospect of seeing the beloved one every night for two blessed weeks. Romance flourished throughout the community during revival time. The gospel singer, a man from another world, was as a rule enjoying single blessedness and was therefore the faint hope of many a maiden heart.

There were at all times several members of our family in the throes of first love, and I approached each revival with the fear that it might result in the loss of a loved one. My only barometer was to watch closely the five older brothers and sister during song service. If they looked straight ahead as they sang,

And he walks with me, and he talks with me,
And he tells me I am his own,

I could relax. But if they gazed understandingly into the eyes of the one sitting snugly by them my heart would sink.

As A CHILD it was with mingled emotions of joy and fear that I came to revival time. That it had some deeply significant bearing on our life was evident by Papa's enthusiasm. The services were long, beginning at eight o'clock and often lasting until after midnight. That was because in reality there were three services in one. First came the song service, of forty-five minutes; then the sermon, lasting at least an hour; and finally the altar service, continuing until the evangelist felt it was the psychological time for closing. The first two were but steps toward the climactic altar service, when sinners came to the mourners' bench to seek salvation.

I delighted in the song service. Sitting on the front pew, swinging legs in rhythm to the music, caroling in supposed harmony but in actual competition with every child—all this was exhilarating, especially when the song leader would say, "Now let's hear just the children on the chorus. Stand up, children, and show these old folks how to sing." Veins would swell out on little throats, childish faces would flush with excitement, and vocal chords would be stretched to bursting as we lifted our heads confidently and shouted,

> Stan-n-n-ding, stan-n-n-ding,
> I'm standing on the promises of God.

But I was uncomfortable during the sermon. I was accustomed to Papa's regular Sunday messages, delivered in the main to his members. While he preached with vim, he seldom pounded the pulpit or raised his voice, as did the evangelist, to "tear a passion to tatters." But

> Wherever God erects a house of prayer
> The devil always builds a chapel there;
> And 'twill be found, upon examination,
> The latter has the largest congregation.

Revival sermons were filled with fire and brimstone, designed to move members of the devil's congregation, who always turned out in large numbers. The fiery furnace with its chamber of horrors was pictured in words that burned into the emotions. The conversion of a hardened sinner is a battle which requires powerful ammunition. I had no way of knowing it was not aimed at me.

Those vivid pictures of flaming punishment to come haunted my dreams, especially since I secretly believed myself to be a sinner. Not that I was conscious of any serious transgression, but I had never been converted. Our Sunday-school teacher had told us the story of Saul's conversion—how on the road to Damascus to persecute Christians he beheld a heavenly light and was blinded for three days, and how after his conversion his name was changed to Paul. I had never beheld a heavenly light and had never been struck blind, and my name was the same as the day I was christened. I had never ever been to the mourners' bench. So it resolved itself into my being a sinner.

Numerous times after the ringing challenge from the pulpit, "What if you should die tonight, would you be prepared?" I impulsively placed one foot in the aisle with the intention of going forward to wrestle with my sins. But the sight of Papa standing there stopped me. I could not face his bewilderment on being confronted with the fact that his baby daughter was a sinner.

Another way out presented itself. In a sermon at our church one Sunday, the bishop had humorously said that when he went to heaven he expected to ride in on Papa's coattail. If the bishop could, I reasoned, so could I. Since I was always swinging on Papa's hand it would be a simple matter when he started to heaven to shift to his coattail. Leaving my corner in paradise to Papa, I thereafter calmly stuffed my ears with cotton and smiled blissfully at the evangelist while he pictured the wages of sin.

Occasionally, however, the antics of the evangelist became so lively that my fingers rushed to my ears to remove the cotton that I might not miss the words that went with such action. I recall vividly one impressive six-foot preacher, who was especially agile. He had a fifteen-foot ramp built on back of the pulpit on which he paced back and forth as he delivered his message, pausing at intervals to draw back a leg and kick it full length and with full force toward the congregation. That was to emphasize the command, "Get out of here, Satan—you and all your schemes!" It had its effect, for Satan and many of his schemes did get out of a large part of the community during that revival.

The fiery sermon, however, was always merely a preliminary to the altar service. Then the very atmosphere became electrified with emotional vibrations.

As the choir sang, Christian people would do "personal work," going in and out among the sinners and quietly talking with them about their souls. I always wished it were possible to catch the words they were saying, but they were invariably muffled by the singing. The next best thing was to watch facial expressions. Earnestness was always etched on the features of the personal worker. At times it would cast a reflected earnestness on the countenance of the lost one. At other times there would be only stark indifference registered there. Often one "under conviction" would need only that word of encouragement, and arm in arm with the Christian he would go to the altar for prayer. Getting the hardened sinners to go to the altar created the tension.

Each night I would choose one person, usually the one who to me appeared the most indifferent, and would concentrate on him. Intently gazing at him, I would say over and over under my breath, "You will go to the altar tonight, you-will-go-to-the-altar-tonight, you-will-go-to-the-altar-tonight." If he did, my ego would give me a self-satisfied pat on the back.

Other children often did personal work, but I could never summon the necessary courage. There were two reasons: I was a sinner myself and therefore disqualified, and my sympathetic heart would stop beating at the thought of how the victim would feel to be singled out as a sinner in a crowd of people.

But Sister was more daring. When she was ten the sins of a little schoolmate who lived across the tracks weighed heavily upon her heart. Seeing her in the congregation one night Sister put on the whole armor of God and wended her way through the crowd to her side.

"Don't you want to be a Christian?" she sweetly whispered into the child's ear.

"——, no!" came the retort discourteous, and with it a hand smack into Sister's face. And clenching her hand for another blow she threatened, "What's more, you git away from me!"

That marked the beginning and the end of Sister's career as a personal worker.

ONE year Papa secured the "Boy Wonder" to hold his revival. Though he was only nineteen years of age, his eloquence attracted crowds to fill the aisles and standing space. He stayed at the parsonage. Every afternoon he paced the length of our front bedroom memorizing and rehearsing word by word his sermon for the evening. Outside his door Candler and I lay flat, our ears planted to the space between floor and door to breathe in his oratory. And when the Boy Wonder raised his pleading voice, "Won't you come place your hand in mine and say that you want to live a Christian life?" we had to restrain ourselves from bursting through the door and shaking his hand.

There is an old saying that "morals are a matter of latitude and longitude." Likewise children's games are a reflection of their geographical and emotional habitat. Children of Southern ministers logically play revival meeting as a favorite game. Every morning during the stay of the Boy Wonder, therefore, an even more boyish Wonder, namely Candler, delivered a fervid sermon behind a soapbox on the back lot, after which we would sing and pray over children of the neighborhood whom we had succeeded in dragging to the mourners' bench.

Behold, We Go Up
to Jerusalem!

JUST as once a year the Jews went to Jerusalem for the Feast of the Passover, so go our preachers once a year to the Methodist Jerusalem—Annual Conference. And although Papa declared that revival-meeting season was the most satisfying of the year, with Conference next in importance, we disagreed. Revival time, and even the excitement of Christmas, paled into insignificance when compared with that week in October each year when we were mentally suspended above the map of Texas anxiously awaiting the time when Annual Conference would drop us on a town in which to settle.

Without the word *conference*, a Methodist vocabulary would not be Methodist. There is the church conference held whenever deemed necessary by the pastor, the quarterly conference when the presiding elder comes to take charge, the district conference when delegates meet at a central church in the district for reports, and finally the climactic Annual Conference, at which the bishop presides.

To me the bishop took on the aspect of a kindly Gulliver towering over the Lilliputian preachers, smiling benevolently down at them, as they crowded around shouting up to him a report of their year's work. Then he would hold them momentarily one at a time in his giant hand, while he scanned the map for a suitable spot in which to put them down, and after giving his blessing, would stride away until the same time next year, when the scene would be reenacted. For on the last day of Conference, after much deliberation on the part of a cabinet made up of the bishop and the presiding elders, appointments are read.

Every preacher waits with bated breath until his name is read, harnessed to the name of a town. This assignment he and his family are to accept and act upon without comment. Under such a system no Methodist preacher is ever without a church, and no church without a preacher.

Papa was, and is, a member of the North Texas Conference, which is one of the five in the state. He has remained in that Conference for forty years and has served eighteen different pastorates. Ours was the Methodist Episcopal Church, South. Explanation for "South" in the name has been humorously explained by some as meaning that we were a little south of God. In truth it was an outcome of the time when Methodists in the North and South refused to see eye to eye on slavery; so those in the North continued to be the Methodist Episcopal Church while below the Mason-Dixon line we became "The Methodist Episcopal Church, South, suh!" Time and intelligence—the Southern part of the intelligence being largely embodied in Bishop John M. Moore—have since united the two, and we are simply the Methodist Church. But the form of government is ever the same, and Conference, as well as October, still comes every year.

EACH YEAR before Papa went to Conference countless things had to be accomplished, and most important was that the "Conference Claims" must be paid in full. "Conference Claims" is a blanket term covering benevolences of the church at large, such as home and foreign missions, the American Bible Society, hospital and orphanage appropriations, educational work, the bishops' fund, and countless other items.

At a local stewards' meeting once, an item mentioned raised an objection. When the list of conference claims was read, ending with "and the bishops' fund," one man's ear failed to catch the final letter on the final word. He rose to a point of order. "Now, Brother Porter," he said, "I want to be a good member of the church and pay my part, but there's one thing I'm not willing to contribute to—that's the bishop's fun. Why can't the bishop pay for his own fun?"

Papa felt nothing short of failure unless he could report at Conference, "Claims paid in full." And to ensure that happy moment he and his stewards would spend every day of the week before his departure visiting church members individually and meet every night at the church to report and plan the next day's campaign.

During that week we went about our activities in a

detached manner, meeting our friends with the
I-shan't-be-with-you-long attitude and rhythmically
dotting every conversation with, "If Conference
moves us . . ." or "If we are here next year. . . ."
The solicitation given those about to be lost forever
was gratifying to us even if we didn't move. Every
request made of Papa would be pigeonholed with the
sentence, "Wait till after Conference." Mother,
preoccupied, would toss back the identical answer to
every question, "Wait till after Conference," until it
seemed that the whole universe was standing still,
waiting till after Conference!

The night before he left Papa would stay and stay at
the church. We dared not go to bed until we knew
whether the report would be, "Paid in full." At about
midnight he would come in, wan and weary. With needle poised in mid-air and with hopeful eyes Mother
would ask, "Did you make it?" and at Papa's smiling
reply, "Paid in full," there would be a ninefold sigh of
relief, after which we could go to our beds, and
Mother could sew the last button on the last new nightshirt for Papa. There were always four of these—the
usual three checked dimity, and one emergency flannel
in the event of a Texas norther. They were made after
the fashion of the day, split up the sides, fitting like a
sack, and reaching to four inches above the ankles.

Papa's wardrobe was new at Conference time, often
the gifts of various members; and at the moment of
departure, as he paraded up and down the room before
us, resplendent in new suit, new shirt, new tie, socks,
hat, and shoes, buttons would pop from the coverings
of nine proud chests. All of us helped with the packing.
It was Papa's habit to bring a gift to each of us, and I

can remember cautioning Mother, "Let's be sure to leave room in the bag for the presents he's going to bring back."

Frequently it was not only Papa's wardrobe which must be new and proper for Conference, but also that of one of the children; for it was our high privilege to go with him when we became eleven years old. It was a mountaintop experience—getting all new clothes at once, riding the train with Papa in exclusive companionship, proudly sitting with him during sessions of the Conference, and being importantly introduced to the other preachers. It did not occur to us that the tedious business sessions were dull. The buildup had been too glowing, and we bravely sat through, telling ourselves it was wonderful. And besides we were missing a whole week of school!

Recently at a family conclave when we were comparing reactions to that journey at eleven years, I asked, "But why did we go at that particular time, the year we were eleven?"

Hugh, the preacher, explained, "Well, Christ conversed with the scholars in the temple at the age of twelve. I suppose it was because our understanding was more developed at that time."

To which Candler retorted, "Understanding, my eye! It was the last year we could ride the train for half fare!"

WHEN Papa returned from Conference with the news that we could settle back into the same groove for another year, there were shouts of joy and blessings on the presiding elder. But if the verdict was that we were to depart immediately, bag and baggage, to live in another town, attend another school, and make other friends—it prompted an indignation meeting. The room was filled with moans and, "How would the presiding elder like for somebody to tell him to move and leave all his friends?" or, "I'd like to tell the bishop what I think!"

In the midst of the lamentations would come Mother's voice, commanding attention by its contrasting calmness, "Now, children, the appointments are only given by the bishop and the presiding elder. They are made by the Lord."

To which there would be a mumbled echo, "Yes, but they could get the Lord's directions mixed!"

But the first pangs of grief were blurred in the feverish activity of getting out of the house before the next preacher's family arrived. Packing was reduced to a minimum. Papa moved himself and his books. Mother's chief concern was the transporting of her private conservatory of plants—coleus, begonias, geraniums, and ferns. As for us, we each made ready his own peculiar treasures. Mother discouraged the accumulation of knickknacks, however, and unless an article was useful or lent some particular beauty she saw no reason to retain it.

Packing over, tearful good-byes were said, individually and collectively, at the farewell party given by church members. With heavy hearts we would ask ourselves, "How can we leave all this behind? Can Janette leave John, Gil leave Marie? Will Raybon ever smile again, torn from Sarah, Ann, Joan, and Lou?" But leave we must and did. And strangely enough, when the golden cord binding us to the past was definitely cut, there came a tingle of excitement at the thought of the future. We were surprised at our own courage, but as Emerson has said, "A great part of courage is the courage of having done the thing before," and this particular thing we had done time and time again. Sturdy little cockleburs that we were, uprooted from one soil, we could easily take root in another.

Our whole thought now was of what we should find in the new place. Would the parsonage be large or small, new or old, well or sparsely furnished? Oh, if only the beds were wooden instead of iron, and if the living-room furniture weren't wicker! Would there be room for a tennis court? And the church—was it run down or in good condition? The church and parsonage were simply a unit in our minds, one as important as the other, and we took equal pride in the appearance which they made to the secular world.

A member of one of the churches tells of the night we arrived in that particular town. The membership had been horrified to learn that the new preacher had seven children—that was before Candler's advent—but they were hoping to take it with grace. In keeping with the custom, several ladies were at the parsonage with a lighted house and a warm supper waiting to welcome the new family. They heard the car drive up, and Miss Bertie stepped out the front door to receive us. The first sight her eyes discerned through the gathering dusk was that of a ten-year-old boy scrambling from the model T Ford, without opening the door. It was Raybon. He hit the ground running and made a complete circle around the church, returning to the running board of the car, before anyone else had time to alight.

"The church is in pretty good condition but needs painting," he reported. "One of the front windows is broken. Seats about three hundred. . . ." He continued until he had given all the facts gathered on his scouting trip, after which the family began to take seriously the business of getting out of the car and inspecting the new home.

THE FIRST day after a move, before a single box was unpacked, Papa would build a swing and playhouse for Sister and me and help the boys lay off their tennis court. He did this to counteract that gone feeling, when it should suddenly engulf us, as it was bound to do. Then he and Mother would begin figuring how to fit their brood into this particular coop. It was usually a problem in higher mathematics, especially if a degree of privacy for each was attained—and Mother insisted upon this. A guest room was out of the question. Since there were only two girls the nicest bedroom was conceded to Janette and me, with strings attached—that it must also serve as guest room.

A part of the equipment of every parsonage was one or two folding beds, the huge wardrobe-looking type that formed a mirror when folded, left the legs dangling in the air as it ascended, and would ascend sometimes without warning or provocation. It could be coaxed to the floor by a vigorous pulling of the legs. Cecil and Hugh, being oldest, were expected to be most sacrificial, and usually wound up folded into the folding bed. Cecil declares that to this day when he is too sleepy at bedtime to be wholly conscious he finds himself groping in mid-air for an iron leg. If after fitting into our assigned places, there was simply too much congestion, Papa and the boys would build a sleeping porch—God's gift to a Texan in the summertime.

Oriented as to spaces, we would then begin to cast our eyes at the furniture. Parsonages were furnished in early years piece by piece from members. When Brother Casteven gave his wife a new chair for Christmas, she would donate the old one to the parsonage, and so furnishings were usually a melting pot of the tastes of the women of the community—after their tastes had changed. In later years, however, furnishings were bought by the Woman's Missionary Society, with the approval of the preacher's wife. It was the responsibility of the Missionary Society to take care of the needs of the parsonage and its wants in so far as they could or were inclined. At their first meeting after Conference, they would give the pastor's wife an opportunity to state those needs.

When Mother returned from such meetings she would be bombarded with eager questions: "Will they get a new rug for the dining room? Will they take the wicker furniture out and buy a divan?" We could always be certain of one treasured piece of furniture. No parsonage afforded this luxury, but Papa considered music as essential to our souls as was food to our bodies, and in the early years he invested in a piano. A possession prized as a member of the family, it was moved to eighteen different towns to sing out its melody.

Ensconced in the new home, we looked to our next bridge to cross from past to present—school. Each system differed from the last, and Papa had to spend the first two or three days at the school building talking for us, like Moses for the Israelites, lest we become

lodged a grade or so behind. Sometimes this happened
in spite of Papa's presence, and there was nothing to
do but bear the shame of going back a grade, through
no greater fault than that of having moved. If we
should be a few chapters ahead of the same grade in
textbooks, we dared not display any such knowledge
under penalty of becoming instantly unpopular with
our schoolmates. It was better to be quiet and give the
impression of slowness to teachers.

After school adjustments came the weekend and our
first Sunday in the new charge. Papa would be on his
dignity, with his unruly hair brushed carefully into
place; and we would be burdened with angel wings,
which could be shed the following week on closer acquaintance.

At the close of the service Papa would say, "Let us
sing number forty-nine. If there are those present who
wish to unite with the church, let them come forward
during the singing of the hymn." As the last stanza
began the entire family would file to the front pew,
overflowing it and causing the new-member recorder
to work overtime. Beginning with Mother, Papa would
call each of our names, then shake hands with us very
impersonally and say, "We rejoice to recognize you as
a member of this church, and pray that you may be
numbered with Christ's people here, and with His
saints in glory everlasting."

BEFORE I was old enough to belong to the church I
could hardly wait till the time when I could be among
the group and solemnly shake hands with Papa in such
formal manner before an audience while he said those
words, ". . . and with His saints in glory everlast-

ing." When I was nine the desire to be a member became overwhelming. As we were moving from one
town to another, I notified Papa that when the family
presented itself for transferring of membership I would
be among those to march up. It pleased him greatly,
and plans were made.

On Saturday afternoon Gil and Candler, jumping
from the roof of a shed which was part of our new
homestead, dared me to follow. I took the dare and
landed with one foot turned under the weight of my
body. Hugh rushed out to pick up a potential church
member with a badly sprained ankle. The doctor
warned, "No walking on that foot for a week." The
older boys made crutches for me. With crutches I
walked, trailing clouds of glory, the envy of Gil and
Candler and our newly made playmates.

At suppertime Papa regretfully said, "Well, honey,
don't grieve too much about not joining the church
tomorrow. You can do that later when your foot gets
well."

My spirits fell. All afternoon I had mentally re-
hearsed the role for tomorrow—hobbling to the front
of the church on crutches, a brave little girl in spite of
her affliction giving her life to the church. And now to
be denied this joy!

Reading despair in my face Mother said, "Why,
Father, I see no reason for her being disappointed.
Two of the boys can carry her to the front, and she can
stand on her crutches while she is being received."

And so it was. When the time came Cecil and Hugh
locked their four hands to their wrists to make a
packsaddle. Stooping long enough for me to sit on it,
they then straightened full height and carried me high

between them down the middle aisle and gently lowered me at the front pew, where Edd stood ready with
the crutches. In my mind I was one of the persons
pictured on my Sunday-school cards following after
Jesus—the lame, the halt, and the blind. And with
double joy I entered the portals of the church on
crutches.

But one memorable first Sunday in a new place, Papa
closed the service without extending an invitation to
anybody to join the church. In his confusion he forgot
everything. There was a reason for his abrupt benediction. At the beginning of the service, when Papa
stepped into the pulpit aware of his new responsibility,
he began, "Brothers and sisters, it is with joy that my
family and I come to live in your midst and to serve
you."

Just then a wave of merriment rippled over the congregation. Papa had no intention of being humorous.
He swallowed and went on, "After the service we
would like to meet each of you personally, and we

want you always to feel welcome at the parsonage.''

Again the congregation smiled and this time their heads turned in unison, while their eyes focused upon an area on the rostrum. Papa continued. "And now for the text. Will you turn with me to the seventh chapter of Matthew, where we find the words of Christ, 'Judge not, that ye be not judged.' ''

At the end of the text, when Papa again raised his eyes, he saw a uniform turning of heads and suppressed smiles. He slicked his hair down with both hands, straightened his tie, and launched determinedly upon his sermon. During his comments on the Scripture, the congregation was alternately attentive and amused. Some sat on the edge of their pews, as if they were expecting something to laugh at; and they were not disappointed, although Papa could only wonder what it was and why this new congregation would not take him seriously. He struggled through the service and quickly closed it. Then he learned the provocation for all the mirth.

One of the vestibules on the pulpit end of the church was unused, and the other was used for the assembling of the choir before the service. On this particular morning when the janitor opened the church, he discovered in the unused vestibule a mother cat with six baby kittens, thoroughly at home and happy. Anticipating the disturbance which kitten meows might cause during the service, he put the whole feline family in the alley. But a mother cat in the alley is a mother still. Undaunted she bided her time and waited for a chance to reestablish her family. It came when the choir marched in and left the door from their vestibule partly open.

Just as Papa took his place at the pulpit, the cat pushed through the opening, dangling from her teeth a sleepy-eyed furry kitten, and walked sedately across the platform back of Papa. Depositing her little one in the home vestibule, she retraced her steps and was soon back with another. Oblivious of her audience, she carried the kittens home, one at a time, silently weaving back and forth behind Papa while the congregation and the choir watched in gleeful speculation as to whether the family would consist of quadruplets, quintuplets, or sextuplets.

AFTER the first Sunday in a new place life would take on a more serene pace, though not an everyday one. There was still the "pounding." On a stated night, soon after the first Sunday, each member of the church welcomed the new pastor, or rewelcomed the same one, with a pound of substance. The pound was accompanied to the parsonage by the donor, "For the gift without the giver is bare." Theoretically poundings were a surprise, but the grapevine telegraph always relayed the news to the parsonage some time before the occasion. Still we had to appear surprised. It delighted my theatrical heart to see the entire family play-acting, registering complete surprise, each time a pound and its giver came through the door. The pound, also theoretical, was more often *ten* pounds—of sugar, potatoes, flour, or corn meal.

Pounds by pounds they came, covering space in the kitchen and overflowing to the dining-room table. The name of the giver was on each gift, scrawled with pencil on the brown paper sack or neatly written on a card tied with a ribbon, pasted on a jar of jelly, or carved

with a knife on a potato or apple. When the crowd had gathered, a strictly unrehearsed program would be given, composed of a take-off on the preacher or stunts about churchgoing. Teasing delighted Papa's heart, and he could give it or take it with equal grace. On pounding night he was all aglow. Like any human being, he enjoyed the assurance that he was esteemed, and he welcomed these pounds as tokens of appreciation.

While the children romped on the lawn the impromptu program for the adults would usually end with a sing-song around the piano, beginning with "Auld Lang Syne," on through such favorites as "Flow Gently, Sweet Afton," and closing with "Blest Be the Tie That Binds."

As the footstep of the last departing guest died away, we would gather to give a close inspection to the giant cornucopia that was our kitchen and to envision weeks ahead when beans and cornbread would play second fiddle. Papa would get pencil and paper to record each contribution with the name of its contributor, as we called out, "Jar of strawberry preserves from the Lanes. Can of lard from Grandmother Neale. Sack of oranges from the Gibsons," and on into the night until we were falling asleep on our feet. But family prayer could not begin until every item, from fresh spinach to pickled pigs' feet, was listed and stored away.

All of us had to be present at the inventory to record mentally what was given by whom, so that we could say when next we met a member, "We are enjoying the macaroni you brought to us," or "I've never tasted better figs than those you gave us." Sometimes we thanked the giver of the figs for the macaroni and the giver of the macaroni for apples, but it was a mistake of the head and not of the heart. A mistake of the heart for me would have been to thank anybody for pickled pigs' feet. None of us liked them, and I could see no reason for giving thanks.

One day soon after a pounding, Candler and I met at the village square Brother Hobson, the donor of a huge jar of pickled pigs' feet.

"Hello children," he said. "We had a mighty good time up at you folks' house the other night." He paused expectantly.

I snapped my mouth together as tight as a clam, determined not to tell a lie. But Candler fed the expectant heart. "Yes, sir. Thank you," he replied. "And I'll bet those pigs' feet you gave us came from your prize pig!"

AFTER the pounding, with life moving along less excitingly, Papa would begin calculating on painting or rebuilding some part of the church property. Although it was an added strain on Mother, she would abet Papa in these plans. If the primary chairs needed painting, she would appeal to the Missionary Society to buy the paint, saying, "I know you feel as I do. I don't want my children to associate religion with shabbiness. The house of God should be shining and bright." And snatching a few minutes out of each busy day, Mother would paint the chairs herself.

Since Papa left no charge that he served without some building improvement, Conference soon began to assign him to the place which most needed some such project carried through. One particular church stands as a monument to his determination. In the face of a large debt, hurdling insurmountable obstacles, with the cooperation of a few stewards he built a dignified house of worship by lovingly handling "every brick" which went into its structure and by persisting when there was nothing left except the will which said, "Keep on."

Papa's building complex afforded us a continuous opportunity for one of the greatest joys of childhood—that of playing around a building under construction, watching the concrete mixer, walking planks on high scaffolding, making footprints on wet cement, and catching some reluctant chicken or dog to make it tread in an obscure corner, thus leaving its imprint to posterity.

Usually it was the church which was reconditioned, but once in our lifetime we knew the supreme elation of moving into a brand-new house and calling it home. Moreover, although it was a parsonage and must house many other families following in our wake, it was built to fit our family. It still stands, a motherly looking house of nine rooms, the lengthened shadow of the only preacher's family numbering more than three children ever to live in it. When we moved to that town, the parsonage was ready to collapse and the congregation ready to build a new one, so Papa set to work drawing up the blueprints. The building committee indulgently granted him free rein in building it as large as, and to whatever plan he pleased.

Their indulgence balked, however, at one request. Being a sociable soul and liking to have large groups of his flock frolic about his home at one time Papa wanted to build the whole first floor of the parsonage into one big party hall, with only a kitchen to keep it company. This evoked a "harumph" from the men on the committee and a quick-spoken protest from the ladies.

"We must keep in mind," said the president of the Missionary Society, "that as time goes on there will be other pastors and other families. One of them might need a downstairs bedroom!"

So Papa acquiesced. A bedroom was included in the first-floor plan, but it was small, and its very walls seemed to apologize for its existence. Quickly, however, it justified that existence by serving as an anteroom where guests might leave wraps on their way to the boastfully spacious living room. And thus the modest little cubicle became unknowingly a forerunner of the fashionable modern powder room.

A house of our own! Proudly we moved into it, and more proudly we lived in it. From the crown of its roof to the sole of its foundation it was new, bright, and unused—from structure to draperies to carpets to furniture. At last we had elbowroom for ourselves and our souls!

For three years we lived in that house, but two of those years I was too harried by one thought to enjoy it fully.

One day visiting me for the first time in our mansion a little friend said with awe, "Gee, Alyene, your family's rich!" And I vigorously nodded in assent. Hadn't we the largest, prettiest, newest house in town? With such a home we had stepped into the privileged class. Contentedly I looked down from my ivory tower upon the less fortunate world.

But a few Sundays later a visiting preacher cast me from my happy pedestal with a verse of Scripture. Ominously he read, "It is easier for a camel to go through the eye of a needle, than for a rich man to enter into the kingdom of God."

As I sat in the family pew with those words ringing in my ears I closed my eyes and raised a petition. "O God, don't let any of us die while we are rich and living in that house." God heard my prayer, and we were spared. But for once I was thankful that there was an Annual Conference to snatch us from the yawning abyss of doom and set our feet once more on the path of heaven. None but Mother knew the reason for my utter relief when, in due time, Conference transported us to a modest five-room cottage in another town.

ONE of the compensations for living this nomad life was the delight of visiting the scene of former habitat. We went often, but Papa went rarely. He maintained that it interfered with the work of a pastor for the former preacher to keep reappearing on the scene; so only upon special occasions and by request did he visit an earlier pastorate.

On one such occasion Papa was called to preach a church dedication sermon. As a prologue to the sermon, he recalled happy days in the community, naming this person and that who had been a soldier of the Lord. Tearfully he came to the name of Brother Gardner. A few months before, Papa had indirectly heard of Brother Gardner's passing. Now he eulogized him, saying, "He has now gone to the glory land, leaving holy footprints on the sands of time—

> Footprints, that perhaps another,
>   Sailing o'er life's solemn main,
> A forlorn and shipwrecked brother,
>   Seeing, shall take heart again."

And in the respectful voice used for speaking of the dead he concluded, "I am sure that all of you, as well as I, miss the blessing of his presence with us today."

Then Papa went into his brief message and at its end sat in the pulpit chair, while the choir sang the closing hymn. Before he ended the sermon it was noticeable that Papa's face had turned from red to white and back to red. Now as he sat his usual dignity was replaced by the shaking of his sides in suppressed laughter. At the close of the song he stepped to the pulpit for an epilogue—this, like the prologue, entirely about Brother Gardner.

"My friends," he said, "I am sure that most of you are aware that Brother Gardner is not in heaven. He is still with us, thank God, sitting with his good wife in the fourth pew." Abandoned laughter burst from the congregation.

Again the doxology presented a graceful way out as Papa said, "Let us stand and sing 'Praise God from whom all blessings flow.' "

The People Had a Mind
to Work

THE Chinese philosopher Lin Yutang has said, "One of the most important consequences of our being animals is that we have got this bottomless pit called the stomach."

The morning after Candler's arrival into our family, there were seven other bottomless pits clamoring, as usual, to be filled. An angel of mercy in the garments of a church member came to the parsonage to mix the mountain of dough for our breakfast bread.

"I use a quart of milk," Mother began, "and twelve cups of flour."

"But Sister Porter," Mrs. Blewett said in amazement, "I've never made that many biscuits in all my life!"

"You needn't worry," Mother said. "They will all be eaten." And they were.

Mrs. Blewett came to our rescue for five mornings, and she was forced to admit that for the satisfaction of seven zestful appetites one pan of biscuits was a mere preamble.

The other six pits, however, bowed in deference to Cecil's, which had snatched the blue ribbon for itself at the tender age of eighteen months. That was also during a time when Mother was ill. Papa had gone to the country and brought back in tow a sixteen-year-old girl, blest with more brawn than brain, to do the housework and to care for Hugh and Cecil. One morning she ambled to Mother's bedside.

"Miz Porter," she drawled. "Cecil's done et seven eggs, an' he's a-pesterin' me fer another 'un. Must I give it to 'im?"

FEEDING her children three times a day was only a minor step in Mother's toeing the mark of the adage "Woman's work is never done." She once said to a neighbor, "I never feel as if I should go to bed at night unless I have made at least one new garment during the day." Cooking meals, making clothing for eight, directing church plays, teaching mission study courses, still at any hour she found the time and energy for feeding the hunger of a childish soul. Her voice with the low, sweet ring of a bell intoning words from the Bible, or from our favorite story books, created an aura of security which no force from an outer world could penetrate.

Papa was necessarily less tangible for reading purposes. Aside from being a shepherd to his flock, there were countless demands on his time in the herding of his own lambs. The alliance between cleanliness and godliness pushed one day out of the week right off his pastoral calendar. On Tuesday Papa the preacher became Papa the laundryman. The mold of tradition which holds Monday as washday was broken, for on Monday morning Papa had to rest from Sunday and in the afternoon attend the Woman's Missionary Society. But come Tuesday each week, the network of clothesline back of the parsonage sagged with the weight of wet garments—numerous enough to clothe a regiment—all done by Papa. For Mother to have the responsibility of washing in addition to her other duties was to his mind unthinkable, and to pay a washwoman for such a task would have been robbing Peter to pay Paul. So by his own efforts, Papa weekly brought the family's cleanliness in step with his own godliness. Flying balloonlike in the wind were ten pairs of long-handled underwear, thirty shirts, ten dresses, fifteen sheets, twenty-five towels, as many cup towels, fourteen pillow cases, and the unlistable odds and ends which complete a family washing.

When that boon to womankind, the washing machine, made its debut, it found joyous welcome in the heart of Papa. He wore out three generations of such machines on one generation of children.

Papa's homework also included the dressing of his progeny each morning for school while Mother prepared breakfast. His scientific mind readily evolved a mass production for the dressing process. We would clothe ourselves according to our talents and then approach Papa at the time he was in motion to fill our particular need. If he was brandishing the hairbrush and our locks were tangled that was the time to step up. If a shoebuttoner was functioning, it was up to us to place our shoes under it at a timely moment.

For one detail of dressing we were all dependent upon Papa—the anchoring of long underwear under our stockings. The trick was to wrap the underwear tightly about the ankle, then sneak up on it with the stocking before it could slip. Papa was a wizard at doing it, though his method was open to objection.

He would take us one at a time upon his lap and seem to lose all consciousness that an anatomy boasted anything besides a leg. The forgotten trunk of the body would be hauled over sideways, tucked under his arm, and pinned down firmly at a forty-five degree angle. The arms waved frantically in search of a straw to grasp, while the upside-down head dangled helplessly near the floor. But Papa would achieve his purpose, and the torso would then be shifted to the other side while a second stocking was pulled into place. When someone else was the victim, the exhibition was fascinating to watch, especially with the added attractions of Papa's facial contortions and the

working of his tongue, as he performed the feat.

"Papa, you're going to have to stop preaching before long," Edd warned him one day. "You're wearing your tongue out dressing your children."

BUT not all work of the household was dispelled by the magic wand of parental hands. "An idle brain is the devil's workshop." Papa literally believed this, and he attempted to outwit the devil by keeping our hearts and our brains and our hands busy—busy with work never too hard but always hard enough. There were assigned duties in the home for each of us, and for the boys jobs outside.

The four older boys first braved the financial world as tillers of the soil. When they were very young, Papa would rent a piece of land for them to farm. It was usually a cotton patch, which he would plow and plant and leave to them to finish.

The money earned when the cotton was sold belonged wholly to them, to be spent as fancy dictated. When out of the corner of his weather eye, Papa could see the money rolling toward a hole, he would rescue it by borrowing the sum and would pay it back with interest when the temptation had passed.

Once when the boys were well launched as cotton farmers, the town toughies became bent on destroying their project. Each afternoon nine dirty-faced, sneering boys would swoop down upon the field to stamp the cotton stalks to earth, scatter and throw dirt on the picked cotton, and commit any other depredation their fertile brains could invent.

Papa had always preached the gospel of turning the other cheek and rigidly held the boys to it. One afternoon, however, he happened to see the injustices of the gang. That night at supper he said, "Boys, the next time that gang bothers you on your own property," and his eyes twinkled, "if you don't clean up on them, I'll clean up on the last one of you."

The next afternoon with bars of restriction down, Hugh, Cecil, Raybon, and Edd were hopefully on guard near a pile of rocks. At least three of them were hopeful.

"It would be just our luck if they didn't show up today," said Cecil.

"Let's hope they don't," Hugh said. For he was a pacifist at heart and had no desire to fight anybody, with Papa's permission or without.

But he hoped in vain. On schedule, Little Napoleon, followed by eight warriors, swaggered into view.

"C'mon, fellers," he commanded, "let's have some fun out of the sissies. They won't fight." And they jumped into the cotton patch like grasshoppers into a wheatfield.

"Who won't fight?" yelled Cecil, his face flaming with antagonism.

"Yea, who won't fight?" chimed in Edd, as he stepped up into the front line beside Cecil, making the most of a chance that comes once in a lifetime.

"Get out of this field and stay out," warned Cecil. And with that he hurled a welter of rocks against the offenders.

"Lookit the preacher's kids," gasped the leader. "C'mon, guys, give it to 'em!"

A heated battle ensued, with rocks as weapons. And although Little Napoleon's forces outnumbered the enemy two to one, he met his Waterloo.

Papa had heard of the fight before suppertime that night, as had the whole town. But he made no comment. At the table during the pause just after the blessing Cecil said, "Well, we whipped that gang today!"

We looked anxiously at Papa to see if he was really glad of it, now that the deed was done. He picked up the platter of bread. "Mother," he said, and we waited with bated breath for his next words, "won't you have some cornbread?" And a contented smile settled over his face.

COTTON in its diverse stages of growth provided many an odd job for the boys. As they grew older and could assume more responsibility, Papa discontinued the renting of land and secured places for them in broader fields of labor. During summer vacation there was always cotton chopping, hoeing, or picking to be done. Of these, chopping was the fastest and most pleasant. Two or three weeks after cotton begins to grow, there comes the necessity for thinning it to a stand. Six or eight stalks are chopped away to every one that is left. Chopping came during the early summer, hoeing after that, and picking in the late summer and fall.

Often Papa would contract for a particular field, and the boys worked by the job instead of by the day. Hence the faster they worked, the better the pay.

When they worked in such manner, if the landscape lacked an adult overseer, Hugh wrapped the mantle of authority about his shoulders and kept the others in line. This he did by virtue of being the oldest and by having formed the habit of taking Papa's place at home when Papa was away.

Life to a little boy is good—even in a cotton patch. Nearly always within sneaking distance was a swimming hole, but how to vanish from sight for a splash in the pond while Hugh's eye covered the field became an exercise of wits for the other three boys.

Chopping in a patch one first day—a sweltering day—they were working near the end of the rows, when before their eyes appeared a mirage. But as they grew nearer, unlike other mirages, it did not vanish. With every step it grew clearer. That joy of joys and thrill of thrills, the cotton rows ran right to the edge of a cool shady creek! The three younger choppeteers exchanged the hopeless glances of the doomed. To pivot at the water's edge and start on another long row was as hard as for a young lover to tear himself from the side of his beloved.

At the end of every row the swimming hole seemed to rise and crook a beckoning finger. Hugh was the only one who failed to see it.

But the God of little boys looked down and placed a parching sensation in Hugh's throat. He also caused the water buckets to be empty, and Hugh had to go to the farmhouse for a drink. As he trudged out of sight, three hoe handles dropped as if by command, and three boys went into a huddle. There was not time for a hasty dip, but there were enough minutes to scheme.

"How can we keep Hugh out of circulation for an hour?" Raybon asked Cecil. For Cecil could usually figure a way to accomplish things—especially a swim.

"Nothing would stop him," said Edd, "but breaking his hoe. If we could do that . . . ."

"We oughtn't to break it," Cecil said, "because he'd know something was up. But, oh, boy! we can sure make *him* break it."

And so the plot was laid. A large rock was carried to Hugh's cotton row and carefully concealed under a clump of Johnson grass. When Hugh's whistle, in re-freshed tones, floated through the air the other work-

ers were too engrossed in their chopping to notice that
he was back. After a brief respite, Hugh lifted his hoe
with more than usual vigor and set to work. There was
for a time only the muted rhythm of four hoes hitting
soft earth. Then came the plotted moment. The stillness was broken by a sharp crash and a splintering of
wood.

"Of all the rotten luck," Hugh called out, "I've
broken my hoe handle." Three pairs of eyes met in
gleeful anticipation. "I'll have to go to the house and
fix it." And once more, as Hugh faded from sight,
three hoe handles dropped to the ground.

On the bonny banks of the creek, clothes were stripped with lightning speed. But the swimming feast was
not to be gulped. First must come the teaser—a little
byplay with wasps. Each boy found a long stick and
according to the customary procedure used it to prod
wasps from their nests in the trees. As the infuriated
insects began to dart here and there, the naked boys
dodged in and out among the trees and stood at last in
defiance on the bank of the creek, until they could
escape no longer the frenzied attack. Then with a
"Yip-pe-e-e!" as the wasps dived at them they dived
into the creek and lay floating in a liquid Elysium.

For the life of him Papa could not understand why it
was taking the boys so long to chop that particular
patch. "I'll just go with them," he told Mother one
morning, "and see what the difficulty is."

He chopped one row. When he came to the end of it
he paused at the edge of the creek. He looked at its
cool, enticing depths. Came the dawn of understanding. He took his hoe and went home.

DURING the school term there were afternoon hours
and Saturdays when the devil might establish a work-

shop. But counteracting jobs were plentiful. It was
never difficult for a preacher's son to find work among
the businessmen of the church. There were always
groceries to be delivered, suits to be cleaned, lawns to
be mowed, ice-cream freezers to be turned at the
drugstore—with a salary of three dishes of cream and a
chance to lick the dasher—cotton seed to be loaded on
boxcars, and other occupations calculated to develop
the sterner stuff of manhood. And there was ever the
church janitorship. If the appointed janitors from the
family were pressed for time some other member
would be drafted for dusting the pews. And when rain
seeped into the basement, as it did on several occasions, it required the combined labor of the entire
family—with buckets and washtub—to bail it out.

Whenever Papa secured a job of delivering groceries
for one of the boys, Edd begged for the privilege of
filling it. One such job, however, was short-lived. For
distributing sugar and flour, Edd was provided a little
wagon drawn by two hardtailed mules called Pat and
Mike. They were young, wild, and determined not to
be controlled by a mere strap of leather. Like all young
creatures, animal or human, they strained and pulled
toward the outside as far as the harness would allow.
Edd got tired of it. "I'll teach you a few things," he
bawled out at them one day, as he pulled them to a
stop near our house. Although he was late with de-
liveries, he unhitched both mules and with coaxing and
pulling succeeded in hitching Pat in Mike's place.
"Now just pull all you want to," he said as he climbed
back into the wagon. They did. The habit of pulling in a
certain direction combined with the stubbornness of
two mules resulted in a grand catastrophe to harness
and wagon. As Edd said "Giddap" and slapped them
with the reins they started pulling—each in his direc-

tion, which now was toward the other. They stumbled over one another, broke the wagon tongue, and made a web of the harness, kicking and stamping all the while. Edd hopped from the wagon and started toward the house. "Pa-a-pa, Papa!" he yelled. "Help me, Papa!"

Papa helped to untangle the mass. But facing his employer was Edd's own responsibility. He lost the job.

As THEY grew older, the boys left the outgrown shells of such occupations for domes more vast. It was while he was chopping cotton that Raybon was informed of a long-distance call from an evangelist, who had heard him sing and wanted him for a gospel singer. He dropped his hoe, and for all he knows it is lying there yet. After that his voice was a greater asset than his hands. Hugh, like Papa, enjoyed a walk down the road of teaching. He interspersed his college years with terms of teaching. After he and Cecil had attended teacher's college for one year. in order to make expenses for going to university, they secured a contract for conducting a two-horse rural school in the blacklands of Texas. Hugh, nineteen years old, was superintendent, teaching the four upper grades. Cecil, seventeen, taught the four lower grades. Two of Cecil's girl pupils in the third grade were older than he, and all of Hugh's boy students were larger than he, since he was short for his age.

It was a tough community, and the pupils had a quaint custom of bidding the teachers farewell with brickbats each year before the term was over. Hugh and Cecil taught their terms out, but not without treading the familiar stony path.

One day Hugh discovered his older boys, a rowdy dozen, chewing tobacco.

"I want to see all twelve of you after school," he told them.

An ominous silence fell over the group—more ominous for him than for the pupils. They looked at each other with smirks and winks, reminiscent of what they had done to other teachers who got out of hand.

After school punishment was meted out in a mass strapping. Cecil came in to lend moral support. He seated himself on the woodpile near the stove with each hand conveniently on a stick of wood. Two braggarts who had boasted what they intended to do to these "slickers" stood nonchalantly cleaning their fingernails with knives. As their time came for passing under the rod, however, they saw Cecil's hand clenched around the threatening sticks of stovewood. Their knives were folded and put away. Hugh presented a comical picture, his height placing him in a perfect positon to hit the proper spot, but his energy ran down like sand from a glass, as he tried to make an impression on the strong frames of the culprits. When the hour was over, the punished boys left in a manner that was almost too docile to forbode any good.

Nothing happened for the rest of that day, but Hugh and Cecil had the sensation of standing on top of a volcano. They could feel the boiling and seething underneath the surface. Next morning came the eruption. As they neared their two-room schoolhouse twelve disgruntled boys and three irate fathers stood waiting in front of the building. A heavy-set black-bearded mountain of a man looking like the giant Goliath stepped from the group. It was Otto Cephas, the father of Leo Cephas.

"Which one of you is Hugh?" he thundered, as he poised a club in air for accurate aim.

Hugh turned white around the gills. But he stepped

out fearlessly. "That's my name," he said in falsetto voice, five keys higher than his usual one, "and don't you dare hit me."

His unexpected resistance was an evident shock to the giant. He began to back away but cursed Hugh with every step. Slapping his pocket, as if it held a gun, he mumbled, "I ought to kill you both."

The other students had crowded around, and it was past time for school to begin. With fluttering heart Hugh "called books," while Cecil climbed back into the buggy and drove to the home of a trustee. The other two fathers evidently lost interest, for they went home. But not Otto Cephas. He followed Cecil, wheel on wheel. Cecil found the trustee, stated his case, and left Otto Cephas in his care. Then he went back to the school building.

Fifteen minutes later the trustee and the father drove into the schoolyard. They summoned Leo from class and took him around to the end of the building, so that the trustee might look upon the welts which the whipping had left on his delicate anatomy.

The building was L-shaped, and from the window in his room, Cecil could see the whole proceedings. The father pulled the boy's pants down to show the marks, but just then Leo saw a girl, who was tardy, coming up the path. He yanked his trousers back up. Intent on what he was doing, the father did not see the girl. He yanked the trousers down again.

"Quit, Pa!" Leo stormed out in irritation, as again he covered himself and held the trousers tightly in place.

"Don't you tell me to quit, you young whippersnapper!" his pa commanded fiercely. "I'll teach you to mind me."

And with that a struggle began between father and

son, which ended with the father's taking his buggy
strap and giving the son a whaling the like of which
Hugh could not have accomplished in a lifetime. They
drove away scuffling and cursing at each other.

The trustee in great relief called Hugh and Cecil outside. "If he ever sets foot on the schoolyard again," he
told them, "hit him with anything you can get your
hands on."

WHEN school was out that year the two boys were
faced with an empty summer. They filled it by selling
Bibles in rural Texas. Having learned a beautiful can-
ned speech embroidered with tear-jerking phrases and
illustrated with a "Wheel of Life," they set out on foot
to scatter truth in the highways and byways. Cecil's
honeyed tones were especially effective with
backwood folks. As he slowly turned the Wheel of Life
and delivered his speech, they would be carried away
on the wings of emotion, and before descending to
earth, they would sign a contract. But when delivering
and collecting time came—the last of the summer—
emotion was spent, and no rural customer was to be
found anywhere.

The Bible salesmen lodged where they could—in
homes in rural communities, or in small-town
hotels—and they called for their mail once a week at a
central post office. Hugh entered the office one day.
"Any mail for me today?" he asked.

"Yep, son, there is," the postmaster reported
gladly. "You got a card from your papa. He wants you
to come home this Sattidy. They're all gittin' along fine
to home!"

With earnings from the sale of Bibles, the boys
bought bicycles, and the following summer they rode

in style through the same territory selling United States maps.

Simultaneously with such occupations of older members of the family, Gil and Candler were in business for themselves—in a lemonade-soda pop stand on the vacant lot next to Papa's city church. They had a thriving trade, though not too much profit, as it was my habit every day to treat my friends. We would be playing lady. "Suppose we drop around to my brother's drugstore," I would suggest in grown-up manner, "and have a dish of ice cream."

Naturally the suggestion would fall on receptive ears; and within the next few minutes Gil, the proprietor, would look up to see a doll caravan—half a dozen little girls wearing wide-brimmed, beplumed hats, trailing dresses, and high-heeled shoes pushing doll buggies down the street toward the "drugstore." With a sigh he would call into action his chief soda-jerker, Candler, and they would serve the party between looks at me which said, "Wait till we get you home." The penalty was somehow never heavy enough to discourage more than momentarily my hospitable impulses. The business eventually went into bankruptcy.

From the time he was twelve years old, each of the six boys from his own earnings clothed himself, provided his spending money, and later helped to pay his college expenses. In addition they pooled a sum which formed an allowance for Sister and me.

Recently I asked Cecil to tell me the various jobs at which he had worked while going through college. I was not prepared for the avalanche.

"Well," he said, "besides the ones you know of, these are the ones I remember: clerking in a dry-goods

store, washing dishes in a restaurant, loading cotton
seed on a boxcar, selling fruit at a Greek stand, milking
a cow and taking care of children for a college professor, selling coal on commission in the middle of summer, substituting for a mail carrier, bellhopping in a
hotel, working on a pipeline in the oil fields, herding
cattle on a ranch. . . .''

There I begged for a breathing spell. His jobs might
be varied in kind, but they were slight in number in
comparison with those of the five other boys.

"THERE IS only one good, that is knowledge," said
Socrates. Papa and Mother heartily agreed with him.
They determined that each of their eight lambs should
eventually have a sheepskin. To that end, thirty years
in all were spent by the family in college. Unable to
sustain several in school away from home, on three
occasions Papa denied himself promotions to larger
churches that he might stay near enough to the university for the children to live at home and commute. And
Conference smiled helpfully at his ambition by station-
ing him at nearby churches.

Somebody was always graduating from something. I
recall one particular June when Candler was graduating from grammar school, I was receiving my diploma
from high school, Janette and Edd were getting B.A.
degrees from college, and Hugh was taking his
Bachelor of Divinity degree. We were all still at home,
all helping Papa carry on the program of his church
next door, and all engaged in some outside work—
even Sister and I, she as a professional church visitor
and I as a teacher of children's class in expression.

It was that year in June, that Uncle Tom came from
Mississippi to visit us. He was a cotton buyer and had
to work only three months of the year. The rest of the

time Uncle Tom took his leisure. He had no particular creed, but like the Hindus, he spent much time in contemplation.

During his visit to us he sat most of the time on the front porch, his feet propped up on the railing, chewing gum and thinking—thinking and watching the endless procession made by a family of ten about their daily activities, going out to school or to work, rushing in to meals or to re-dress, and rushing out again to work, or to play, or to church.

One afternoon when the stream of traffic across the porch had been unbroken, he heard the screen door slam one more unbearable time. This time it was Papa, his Bible under his arm, quickly shoving his watch back in his pocket and adjusting his hat as he hastened across the porch. Uncle Tom could stand no more. He banged his feet to the floor from the railing and stood up in exasperation.

"Great Scott! Edwin," he shouted to Papa, who by that time was crossing the yard, "when do you people *Meditate?*"

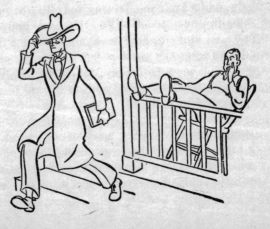

They Twain Shall Be One

"THOSE whom God hath joined together, let not man put asunder." Papa was intoning the words with a dignity suited to a flower-banked altar, glowing candlelight, and a bride in a flowing veil. But the picture fell short in a few details. The bride wore houseshoes, a flowered kimono, and the expression of a frightened fawn. The groom wore brogans, overalls, and a cat-that-swallowed-the-canary look. Papa was full-suited, although he had dressed with the speed of a fireman answering his first call.

It was February and three o'clock in the morning. There were no flowers, and the only wedding music was the rhythmic chatter of teeth—those of the three principal figures, quivering through the rites, and those of Sister and me, dragged from a warm bed to serve as witnesses. The law demanded two onlookers at a wedding ceremony, and rarely did the persons getting married bring them. This couple had none, as they were obviously staging an elopement.

The groom urged, "Make it short as you can, preacher. Just so it's legal."

And Papa began, "Dearly beloved, we are gathered together . . . ." As he continued through the ceremony, the harassed groom, instead of bestowing loving glances upon his bride, kept his eyes glued on the door and an ear cocked to the air.

At the words "I pronounce that they are husband and wife" the groom, without waiting for the final blessing, thrust two dollars into Papa's palm, picked up his stolen bride, and carried her over the doorstep.

Papa held the lamp high in the doorway to lend light, as we watched them. The husband flung his wife upon a horse, untied the steed, and mounted to the saddle in front on her. She placed her arms around his waist, snuggled her head against his back, and they galloped through the night.

We had no sooner pulled the covers up to our ears than there came a pounding on the front door and shouts to waken the dead. The pajamaed and nightgowned household rushed to the living room and stood terrified, while Papa unlocked the door. After one turn of the knob a colossal, red-faced figure with a gun burst into the room. His head was stuffed into his neck, his nightshirt stuffed into his trousers, his trousers stuffed into his rubber boots, and the whole stuffed into a mackintosh. Between puffs he demanded to know if Papa had married two young fools. Papa tremblingly admitted that he had. Then as we fought for clinging space on Mother's nightgown, the presence leveled his gun at Papa.

"Parson," he roared, "I'm gonna git that pair, an'
you can untie that knot as you tied it," and he moved a
step nearer. "For thirty-one years I've kept any low-
lived man from carryin' off my daughter, and I'll be
hornswoggled if Jasper Fox can outslick me—even if
he is forty year old!"

With that he banged out the door.

We stood transfixed from fright. "He won't be
back," Papa said, as he calmly locked the door. And
we went once more to our beds, sighing with the sheer
peace of being too young to marry, since it was so
much trouble, and since one had to freeze to death to
do it.

"It is alleged . . . that such as are in the institution
wish to get out and such as are out wish to get in." To
the clerical eye of a preacher's family, it seems that
everybody is storming the gates to get in.

A wedding ceremony, like mercy, droppeth as a gen-
tle rain from heaven upon the parsonage beneath. Nobody can predict the hour. It is twice blest: it blesses
the preacher who gives the vows and the couple that
takes them—it is also alleged.

Almost two centuries ago William Cowper advised
young lovers to

> Choose not alone a proper mate,
> But a proper time to marry.

A few wise ones take that advice and set a proper
wedding date, but for many the proper time is when a
"yes" can be coaxed from the lips of the beloved—and
a preacher caught on the wing.

Papa's wedding ceremonies ranged from high church to high buggy seat, from high noon to midnight, and from high fee to no fee at all.

We were thoroughly trained in the technique of receiving wedding parties. It was not difficult to recognize them. However ordinary the man, however commonplace the woman, there is a radiance from their beings, when they have touched the hem of divinity and are transformed by love.

It was our duty to give couples, however unexpected, the impression that Papa was in readiness for them. We were cordially to invite them in, make them comfortable, and then excuse ourselves to inform Papa of their arrival. If a search of the other part of the house or the study did not bring him to light, we reported to Mother. She usually knew where he was. She would send one of the boys posthaste out the back way to the grocery store, or to Grandma Steele's, and before the couple could become impatient and start on a hunt for another preacher, Papa would come smiling through the front door.

The linking together of two people for the remainder of their lives was to Papa an important stitch in his ecclesiastical knitting. The gravity of each ceremony made such an imprint on his face that any uninformed witness would have guessed him to be the bridegroom. He never learned to take a wedding casually. The outward sign of that inward feeling was seen in his habit of making some special preparation for each ceremony. Although he might be dressed in Sunday best when the couple appeared, they were kept waiting while he went through a brief ritual, if nothing more than changing his tie or brushing his hair.

Papa had difficulty in finding a topic of conversation to bridge the gap from this mundane world to the rarefied heights where dwell two people about to be married. First there were naturally introductions all the way around. Then came the pause that depresses. Papa would break it by saying, "My, what fine weather we are having," and the groom would agree, "We certainly are," and there would come another pause. Papa would say, "It looks as if the crops will be good this year." Someone would agree. Finally, as the silence was becoming embarrassing, with one fell swoop of courage, Papa would look into space somewhere between the bride and groom and say, "Whenever you are ready."

Poor things, when they had been ready and waiting these many minutes! They would look at each other and shyly stand side by side. Almost every time Papa had to ask the groom to stand on the other side. And the ceremony would begin.

In contrast to his groping for words before the ceremony, after the *Amen* Papa usually became garrulous. The tension over and congratulations given he would insist that the visitors sit with us for a while, as he talked on and on. But the newlyweds were always eager to attend to that last detail, the paying of the fee, and say their good-byes.

One day when Papa came to the final part of the ceremony, declaring, "Forasmuch as John and Sara have consented together in holy wedlock, . . . I pronounce that they are husband and wife . . ." John, who had been gazing at the floor to that time, looked out of the corner of his eye at Sara. She smiled into his glance, and their eyes were only for each other for several heavenly moments. They were so transported that they failed to hear the *Amen* and failed to hear Papa's clearing of his throat to notify them that the ceremony was at an end.

"Ah," thought we, who were looking on, "there is real love."

Papa grasped the hand of the groom and began to pump it up and down in a hearty congratulation, which brought the pair back to consciousness. He asked them to sit. They did not sit, and they did not go. They continued to cast sheepish grins at each other.

"I hope you'll be happy," Papa said, although he had told them the same thing five minutes before.

"Yes, sir," said John self-consciously, and at last nerved himself for the question he had been putting off. "What do I owe you, preacher?" he asked.

"Oh," said Papa with his usual reply, "whatever you think your wife is worth."

The witnesses could have been brought low with a feather at the response. Reaching into his pocket John jangled some coins. Then he brought one out and, with all seriousness, asked, "Have you got change for a quarter?"

Quite different was the response of another bridegroom. When he asked the same question and Papa gave the same reply a twinkle came into his eye. He rammed a hand to the depth of each pocket of his trousers and quickly turned those cavities inside out, dislodging bills, quarters, dimes, and pennies in a jumbled array. Without counting, he handed it to Papa—to the last penny. "She's worth all I've got," he said.

ONE evening at dusk a buggy drove up in front of the house. In it lolled a rural Jeanie with light brown hair, and by her side was Harry with light brown jeans.

They gave the impression of going nowhere in particular. The buggy wheels made one final poky revolution and then stopped. Harry called out to Edd, who was playing in the yard, "Is this where the Reverend lives?"

"Yes, sir," Edd responded, his trained ear catching the tinkle of wedding bells. "Won't you come in?"

"Naw, just tell 'im to c'mere," he said. "We wanta git hitched, but we don't wanta git out."

Papa came out. "Don't you think we might have a nicer ceremony in the house?" he asked. For he preferred a dignified rendition of any pastoral service, especially a wedding.

"Naw, we'll jist set here," said the groom. The bride seemed to have no say in the matter.

"As you wish," Papa agreed.

By that time a flock of neighbor children had formed a gaping audience. "Edd," said Papa, "go tell Hugh to light a lantern and bring it here. It's getting dark. And bring my ritual."

I never could understand why Papa must always read the wedding ceremony from the ritual. I knew for a fact that he was the smartest man alive, and any person, smart or otherwise, should know by heart a thing he has said as many times as Papa had said those words. True he did not often look on the page, but for some reason he had to hold the book in his hand.

Edd came, bringing the ritual; Hugh came, bringing the lighted lantern; and the rest of us came for no reason at all.

"Dearly beloved," said Papa, "we are gathered together here in the sight of God, and in the presence of these witnesses"—chance witnesses they were, with dirty faces, yet duly solemn—"to join together this man and this woman in holy matrimony."

The groom sat in a sprawling position, with one foot propped negligently on the dashboard and twisted one of the reins around his finger. The bride stared off into the darkness. Somehow they lived through the final words.

Then a heavy sigh escaped from the lips of the groom, in relief that the ordeal had ended. It was sympathetically echoed by the youthful audience. The neighbor children thought it was all over, but not so the preacher's children. We knew there was one other little matter.

"Have you got a blank check, Reverend?" drawled the new husband.

"Yes, sir," said Papa. "We have two banks, you know. Which one?"

"Oh, either one," he replied with convincing braggadocio.

Cecil was sent to the house for a check, and it was made out by the groom for an ample sum.

"Thank you," said Papa, folding the check into one hand, as with the other he congratulated the groom and shook hands with the bride. "I hope you'll have a happy life together." And the bridegroom picked up the reins and drove away.

As the buggy melted into darkness, Hugh, still holding the lantern, took the check from Papa's hand and held it up to the light. "I'll be bound it's no good," he said (we were not allowed to say "I'll bet"). "You know he doesn't have money in two banks."

"Now, son," said Papa, "judge not. He may be a thrifty boy. And it's a pretty good thing to keep your money in different banks; if one fails, you're not so hard hit."

Hugh took the check in to Mother, who also cast a doubtful eye when she heard the story; but she said never a word.

A few days later as we sat down to the noon meal, the local banker stopped by to see Papa. He hummed, and he hawed, and at last he got around to the point of his visit.

"Brother Porter," he said, "I have a check here. We can't seem to locate this account."

Across the table Hugh's eyes met Mother's in understanding, and into the realm of the might-have-beens went Mother's new fall dress.

A FAVORITE sport of the family was guessing wedding fees. Almost without exception, victims of the matrimonial net dallied a bit getting out of the buggy or car, prolonging the last few moments of freedom. If they did approach the door readily, time was spent in the preliminaries—locating Papa, or waiting while he prepared for the ceremony. This interval gave ample opportunity for sizing up the pair and speculating on the amount of the fee they would pay. Emily Post's predecessor fixed the minimum amount at three dollars, but few seemed to have read the book of etiquette.

It simplied a three-dollar guess for us to whisper, "They've read the book." Cecil tacked a scoreboard in the hall, where we could mark up our entries. Whenever a couple approached with the marriage gleam in their eyes, guesses would be made by as many as were at home, and after the ceremony whoever had guessed closest wheedled Papa out of the fee. That became a problem, however, as the boys were earning their own spending money and Sister and I had no such opportunity. So it was agreed that the fees would take turns among Mother, Sister, and me. But the sport of guessing continued.

When Papa had to be at the church in the evening, I went to my bed and to sleep without question. But if he was home, nothing would satisfy me except to sit in his lap, while over my sleeping form he read his evening paper. One winter evening after a rare Texas blizzard, when ice covered the streets and crackled in the trees, I was snugly nestled in Papa's lap for the evening. There was a knock on the door. Outside stood two men and two women.

"Could you perform a double wedding right away?" one of the men asked.

"Certainly," Papa said, and invited them in to warm themselves by the fire.

"We know it's cold and the church is not heated," said one of the prospective brides, "but we'd feel much better about it if we could have the ceremony in the church." She did not add, but we understood, that people being married did not mind the cold or ice or any other worldly discomfort.

Papa sent Hugh ahead to turn on the lights and to remain as a witness. As the others were all studying, I begged to be the other witness. I remembered it was my time to get the fee. Mother reluctantly consented. "I'm afraid you'll take cold," she said, "but maybe not, if I wrap you up well." She bundled me up like a stuffed teddy bear, and I swung to Papa's hand, as we went to the church.

I ecstatically anticipated the fee. Being only eight years old, I had some difficulty in figuring the exact amount. But I could multiply. Now here were two weddings. If each man paid two dollars that would be four dollars! And if people put Papa to a lot of trouble to marry them, they sometimes paid him twice as much. This was a lot of trouble. Two times four dollars would be—two times one is two, two times two is four, two times three is six, two times four is eight—eight dollars! And all my own! That would buy a new doll, two new books, that pair of red-topped shoes—, my childish millennium had come.

It was cold in the church, and our breath made smoke when we exhaled. I sat close to Hugh, as we witnessed.

Came the part of the ceremony that I always dreaded, "Therefore if any can show any just cause why they may not be lawfully joined together, let him

speak, or else hereafter forever hold his peace." What if someone should speak up and say, "I know reasons why they shouldn't be married"? No one ever had, but with every wedding there was that possibility. And there was the even more tense moment when the bride or groom might confess—"I require and charge you both (as ye shall answer at the dreadful day of judgment . . .), that if either of you know any impediment why ye may not be lawfully joined together in matrimony, ye do now confess it . . ." That always sent a chill down my spine. "Oh, don't let anybody confess an impediment, whatever that might be!" I breathed this time. "Now now, with my eight dollars in the balance."

Nobody objected, nobody confessed, and the ceremony proceeded as usual to its conclusion.

The double wedding called for a twofold kiss and fourfold handshaking. This time, as he shivered with cold, Papa did not seem to mind the early departure of the party. There were no questions of "what do I owe you?" But my watchful eyes saw each groom drop something into Papa's hand, and a disappointed ear heard the clink of coins. Still that might be silver dollars instead of bills.

When the two couples had gone, and Hugh was ready to turn out the lights, Papa dropped the fee into my hand. Before the lights went out, I had just enough time to see that it was five quarters! Five quarters and nothing more! I was sorry that I had wished them happiness.

AT one charge the parsonage was particularly sparsely furnished. Crops had not been good for the past three

years. Church theatricals and box suppers had failed to
make money for the Missionary Society. So it was
agreed that all wedding fees for the year should go to
Mother for improvements on the house. Especially the
dining room. It was the shabbiest room of all, and the
most used for company. The chairs were frazzled to a
shamefaced state.

When Mother heard of the approaching marriage of
Lena Blanton to a wealthy man up North, her heart
gave a leap. That would surely bring in such an elegant
fee that combining it with the nest egg we already had,
we could get the dining-room chairs all at once. The
day after Mother heard the news she went to the local
furniture store to look around. "We hope to get some
chairs for the parsonage in the near future," she told
the merchant.

Great preparations were made for Lena's wedding.
The town was all agog. Few people knew that she even
had a sweetheart, for she had met and become engaged
to him while visiting in New Hampshire. And now he
was coming all the way to Texas to marry her. The
morning of the wedding, ladies of the church gathered
flowers from every yard and from the hillside to dress
the little chapel in spring colors. It was bluebonnet
season, and armloads of Texas bluebonnets were
banked to create a background for the ceremony.

The hour was set for four o'clock in the afternoon,
and the town was set to witness the ceremony. But at
two o'clock the railroad station agent came riding up to
our door on his bicycle and asked for Papa.

"B-b-b-brother Porter," he stuttered, "a t-t-t-
telegram just c-c-c-came from Miss Lena's feller." His
eyes opened wider. "It seems he ain't a-goin' to

m-m-m-marry her after all."

Papa took the telegram and put it into his inside pocket. He got into his buggy and drove the three miles to the Blanton home to break the news gently to Lena.

After he had gone, Mother's sympathetic heart grieved and overflowed through her eyes. As she walked about bewailing the frailties of men, she subconsciously found her way to the dining room. There we saw her as she sank into one of the worn-out chairs. "Poor Lena!" she sniffled, and dabbed her eyes. She abstractedly rose and moved about the room. "Poor Lena!" she said again as she absentmindedly sat on another one of the frayed chairs. "Poor, poor dear!"

Poor Lena survived, but poor Mother was crushed with the teasing when we told Papa how sorry she had been for the jilted bride, and where she had sat while she wept for her.

A GIANT moon shines over Texas. Nowhere does the moon look larger or shine brighter than in the Lone Star State. And with the bright moon during spring and summer months, the wedding industry flourished. Saturday afternoon and evening always afforded one wedding at our house, and not infrequently there were several.

To the neighbor children, we lived in a chosen world where exciting events took place. They were forever seeing a man and a women go into our house to get married and come out to ride away, and they were forever wishing that they could see the weddings. Candler hit upon the idea of letting them peep into that chosen world for a nominal fee. So the window-shade theater was established—showing only weddings.

Every time there was to be a ceremony, Candler rounded up the would-be spectators and Gil collected ten cents from each of them. When they had paid and were planted in darkness outside the living-room windows in looking position, I would go into the house, nonchalantly stroll about the room, and raise the shades. With Gil as chief silencer the audience would take in the show. After the performance, the three of us would divide the proceeds, all without Papa's knowledge.

On one of those Saturday nights, when a child audience peered in from the darkness, a man and a maid stood taking their vows. The groom was all attention, but the bride stood with amazing unconcern through the whole procedure, until the ring ceremony. The best man took the ring from his pocket and handed it to the groom, who handed it to Papa, who handed it back to the groom, who placed it on the bride's finger. The bride had watched intently that circle.

"Please repeat after me," said Papa to the groom. "With this ring I thee wed."

"With this ring I thee wed," he began. At that point the bride was unable to stifle her enthusiasm longer. This was obviously the first ring she had ever owned. She raised her hand to a distance and gazed proudly at the ring.

"I know it's pure gold," she burst forth, "or it would a-wore out with all that passin'!"

WAS there ever a wedding without some unforeseen happenstance? Can a bride forget her attire? I remember one frail girl who had a distressing time. It was at one of those unexpected weddings in our living room. She was a shy little thing, trimly gowned in tailored crepe. We had the impression that to herself she was saying, "I hope I live through it." The groom, as in most cases, seemed much more confident.

As Papa was chanting, ". . . in holy matrimony; which is an honorable estate . . . ," her hand moved surreptitiously to her back and gave a yank to something in the region of her waist. The ceremony continued. Came the prayer, "O eternal God, . . . send Thy blessing upon these Thy servants, this man and this woman . . ." The bride reached again to her back and gave another yank. The prayer ended, ". . . and live according to Thy laws, through Jesus Christ our Lord."

As Papa said the *Amen* the girl, thinking it was the end of the ceremony instead of only the end of the prayer, took a deep breath. That was her undoing. The string around her waist broke, and to the floor fell a ruffled petticoat. Her face flamed in embarrassment, as Papa went right on with the ceremony. Mother slipped around behind her and tugged at the petticoat. She stepped out of it, and Mother smuggled it under a sofa pillow. Blessed Mother! The groom was spared the too-sudden disillusionment of learning that instead of an angel from heaven, he had wedded a human being who wore petticoats.

OFTEN our assistance in performing weddings lay in other duties than in being witness. There were sometimes superfluous members of the wedding party to be entertained on the front porch or the lawn. Such as one Saturday afternoon, when the groom placed his brood of six on one side of the walk, and the bride her four children on the other, with warnings to be quiet till they were summoned.

During the solemnity inside the two forces outside staged a battle royal. As Papa prayed that the pair might "ever remain in perfect love and peace," there arose a shout from the front yard, "Mama, Mama, make this bully leave me alone. Mama-a-a-a!"

The ritual was interrupted while the mother and father came to the lawn and effected a temporary truce between their offspring. Then they went back into the house for the final blessing, and the wedding formation moved on to resume maneuvers on other battlefields.

As WE sat around the fire one winter evening, schoolbooks littering the floor and tables, there came a knock upon the door. Papa opened it to admit Brother Benedict, a lifetime member of the congregation.

"My wife and my niece and her fiancé are in the car," he said. "You know, Mary and I were married in this parsonage thirty-five years ago, and our niece has set her head on being married tonight in the very same room."

"We'll be glad to arrange that," said Papa.

"We didn't know just what you'd think of it," Brother Benedict continued. "When the parsonage was remodeled nine years ago some of the rooms were shifted about. The room we were married in is now your kitchen."

Papa looked thoughtful. He had never performed a kitchen ceremony.

"I told Jenny you might not want to do it, but she wouldn't be satisfied till I'd asked."

"Tell them to come in," said Papa. "It's a bride's privilege to be married where she wishes. We'll have the wedding in the kitchen."

Mother put down her book and indicated with a look that she wished the help of Sister and me in making a lightning transformation of the kitchen.

The whole family witnessed the ceremony. It took place before an improvised altar—the kitchen sink with strands of ivy hanging over its side, a pot plant in the window above, and a lighted candle on each of the drainboards. The bridal party entered to the strains of drip, drip, drip, from an obliging water faucet. "I Love You Truly" was sung by Mother's proud canary, and as Papa concluded, ". . . the Lord mercifully with His favor look upon you," the groom gave his beloved her bridal kiss over the kitchen sink. If it is true what they say about the way to a man's heart, this clever bride, by plighting her troth in the kitchen, was a milepost ahead, shooting straight for the mark.

AFTER one wedding which Papa performed, the talk of the guests was not what the bride wore and how the groom acted, but what Cecil did not wear and how the groom failed to act.

Edith Meadows had been an active worker in the church for several years, teaching a Sunday-school class and singing in the choir. Now she was marrying a Mr. Charles Abel from out of town, whom few townspeople had seen. She graciously invited all of her friends to witness the ceremony at the church.

"We feel that it is the dawning of happiness for both of us," Edith told Papa, "so we wanted to be married just as day is dawning."

The afternoon before the ceremony the little church was garmented in beauty such as it had never known. The altar was banked with greenery and flowers, accented with garlands of fern imported from a florist in a nearby city. All night the little church stood in readiness for the moment at dawning when it could put its best foot forward to open a bright way for one of its loved children.

It was still pitch dark the next morning when Papa stood over the bed where Cecil and Raybon were sleeping. Cecil was the official church janitor, and it was his duty to give the final touch to the preparations.

"Son, wake up," said Papa, shaking him out of a dream that had nothing to do with janitoring. "You'd better go over right away and turn on the lights. It's only forty minutes until the wedding, and some of the guests might be coming."

"Awright," Cecil drowsily replied. Why would anybody pick such an unearthly hour to be married?

It was late spring, and the nights were warm. Cecil had discarded his pajamas in favor of a cooler sleeping garment—his B.V.D.s. There was only a step out our back door to the church study, and it was not even light yet. As Cecil intended to go back to bed to get the last forty winks, he did not bother to dress. Half asleep he rolled out of the bed, went out the door, and into the door of the church. He fumbled his way through the study and across the rostrum to the opposite side of the choir loft to the master switch, which turned on every light in the church. In the dark he found the handle and pulled it down, flooding the church with light.

As he yawningly turned to retrace his steps, his

eyes, which had been only half open, popped out on unbelieving stems. For scattered here and there in the auditorium were *people*—wedding guests who had found their way to seats through the darkness of the church and were awaiting the hour. Now they sat forward in amazement and merriment at this unexpected eye opener. The floor would not open up and swallow Cecil, as he wished it would, and there was not even a near exit through which he could vanish. He placed his hand on the light switch again, plunged the world and himself into comforting darkness, and made his embarrassed way out the door.

"Hey, Cece," followed the laughing voice of a masculine spectator, "I didn't know we were having flower girls and everything."

With burning cheeks Cecil crawled back into bed and roused Raybon. With the promise of a magnificent bribe, Raybon dressed and turned on the lights at the church again.

Thirty minutes later Papa stood with the best man in the study, ready to begin the ceremony. The church was packed. Edith, in the vestibule, was starry-eyed and radiant, basking in the expressed admiration and the unexpressed envy of her bridesmaids.

The pianist sat with hands poised over the keys, and the soloist stood by her side.

> When the dawn flames in the sky,
> I love you-u-u-u.

Music filled the expectant hush. Papa turned nervously to the best man. "Where is Mr. Abel?" he asked.

"I was just wondering about that, sir."

"He'll have to be here in five minutes," said Papa, "or he'll hold up the ceremony."

Two minutes passed. The song was over. It was time for the *Lohengrin* march and the entrance of brides-maids.

"Surely he's about somewhere," said the best man.

"You'd better go around and see Miss Edith," Papa told him. "Tell her to wait till we find him."

The pianist was playing "Here Comes the Bride" and one bridesmaid was already moving down the aisle when the best man made his way to Edith.

"Charlie hasn't shown up yet, Edith," he told her. "Do you know where he could be?"

The stars in her eyes went behind clouds. "Why, no. He left my house at midnight. He's staying at the hotel."

"Well, don't march in till we tell you to," he said as he darted out the door to go around the church and relay the message to Papa.

"Go find one of my sons in the audience," Papa told him, "and send him to the hotel to see if Mr. Abel is there."

Edd was the most available son. He sped to the

hotel, which was only three blocks away.

"Is Mr. Charlie Abel staying here, Brother Wren?" he asked the man back of the desk.

"Why, yes, Edd, but I reckon he's already at the church. He's gettin' married this morning, you know."

"Well, he's not there." Edd was halfway up the stairs. "What's his room number?"

"Room number nine, son."

Dashing down the hall to number 9 Edd banged on the door. "Mr. Abel, Mr. Abel!"

"Yes, whaddya want?" a sleepy voice grumbled.

"It's time for your wedding," Edd panted. "The people are waiting. Music has already begun. What must I tell them?"

"Holy smoke!" The voice was less sleepy now. There was the thud of two feet hitting the floor. "Tell them to hold everything. I'll be right there!"

Edd covered the three blocks in minimum time. The piano was still repeating "Here Comes the Bride."

"Hold everything," Edd reported to Papa. "Behold, the bridegroom cometh!"

Dawn, the ever punctual, would not stay her feet even for such a romantic cause, and sunlight, "not to be suppressed," overflowed the world as Edith Meadows placed her hand in that of Charlie Abel and Papa laid his hand over the clasped ones, saying, "I pronounce that they are husband and wife."

As ONE man and woman sat in the parsonage waiting impatiently to be married Sister and Gil were exchanging small talk with them, until Papa could get redressed.

"I've just put some splints on the wing of a bird,"

said Gil. "It fell from a tree. I guess it will be all right now."

"I'm sure it will be," the bride responded, just to be polite.

"When I grow up I'm going to have a hospital of my own," Gil went on.

The groom fidgeted. He was not interested in what was going to happen to a little boy he had never seen before. He looked over at the piano. "Wouldn't it be nice," he said to his bride, "If we could have a song before our wedding?"

Sister, eleven at the time, was trained to respond to any request to play or sing. "I'll be glad to sing for you," she said sweetly.

Importantly walking to the piano stool she seated herself and fixed her skirts just so. And as Mother in the back bedroom gave Papa's hair a final lick with the brush, to her unbelieving ears floated Sister's voice sweetly crooning "Meet Me Tonight in Dreamland."

Ways of Pleasantness

WHEN the older boys were young and Papa's pastorates were in West Texas, their outlook upon life was tinged with the wild-west atmosphere which pervaded the towns. The small towns were secondary to the large ranches that surrounded them. Professional broncho busters ambled up and down the streets; cowboys lolled in front of the drugstore; ranch owners strode importantly through the town square smoking long cigars; ten-gallon hats, spurs, and high-heeled boots were regulation garb for the masculine contingent. Farmers brought their bucking horses to town, and the broncho busters broke them in, right in the middle of the town square. The horses would rear and cavort, while the busters hung on for dear life, shouting epithets in the ears of the beasts and finally subduing them. All of which would appeal to that capacity for high adventure and hero worship in the soul of every boy. It made its due impression on the four in the parsonage.

In one town they could sit in their own hayloft and get a bird's eye view of the goings on. They noted the swagger of the busters, they studied their technique of riding, and they memorized their lingo. Then they practiced it in the cow lot.

One Saturday afternoon when the town square was thick with human beings milling about, the boys decided to carry their broncho busting to its rightful place—the town square.

Only Molly, the cow which gave our milk, and her calf Daisy were available for busting. Pushing Molly into the narrow hallway of the barn, with much effort the boys succeeded in tying a saddle on her. The calf was to be ridden bareback.

Hugh mounted Molly, and Cecil mounted the reluctant Daisy, while Edd and Raybon gave a literal interpretation of the term "cowpunching." Round and round the lot they went, punching the two cows mercilessly, until bovine irritation was at a high peak. When Molly began to bellow and try to buck the saddle off and Daily was snorting and pitching, the gate was opened and the rodeo troupe charged through. They rounded the corner, the boys whooping and yelling, the cows pawing and bellowing.

The Saturday crowd began to scatter, as the two wild cows with boys astride came forging through the street. Proudly exhibiting his newly acquired lingo Cecil yelled into Daisy's ear, "Git around there, you pie-eyed, locoed son of a lop-eared rabbit! Drat your dog-gone hide!"

Papa was standing on the street corner in conversation. "Sh-h-h-h!" he expostulated, as the startling scene whizzed by, and took out after them in a long run, his coattail flapping in the wind. "Stop, boys! Stop!" He shouted, sprinting his way around the square. Enjoying the excitement, the crowd took sides, some betting on the preacher, some on the kids.

Papa's long legs enabled him finally to overtake them. He got Molly by the horn and Hugh by the ear and told the others to follow. They did, slowly and meekly. It was a subdued rodeo which completed the square and ignominiously rounded the same corner and entered the same gate through which it had burst upon an unsuspecting world with such fanfare and Ringling Brothers showmanship only a few minutes before.

ALTHOUGH cards and dominoes were banished from the compass of our experience, they were not mourned. Trying to find an hour for a game of cards in the overcrowded schedule of our days would have been as fruitless as the search of Diogenes for an honest man. With school, church meetings, houseguests, work, and outdoor play, days were filled to overflowing.

The boys had bicycles, which they bought with their own earnings. I could ride them when Papa wasn't looking, but only sideways, through the bars. My short legs would not reach the pedals sitting astride a high bar on a boy's bicycle. I begged for one of my own. The bank account was never overfull, however, for buying such a treasure; and besides, Papa considered it tomboyish. "I won't ask for a bicycle any more," I told him, "If you will let me have a dog and some skates."

The dog was granted, and before long I was cuddling to my heart a fluffy white spitz pup. The skates were longer in materializing. Papa had misgivings about them. Skating rinks were frowned upon by church members, and while my skates would be used only on the sidewalk, still few children of the church members owned them. Mother brought pressure to bear, however, and on my ninth birthday I gleefully hugged in one arm a pair of shining skates and in the other my dog Donnie.

As I sailed up and down the walk and around the church hour after hour, joy was unconfined—until the day Papa's misgivings took human form. A steward on the official board who had dyspepsia in body and gout in the imagination turned into our yard. My chum and I were sitting on the front steps, noisily clanking our skates in preparation for the afternoon's fun when he approached. With a disapproving glance he said, "Could I see your Papa? It's a little matter of personal business."

I dropped my skates to the step. "Come in and sit down, please," I said, trying to be polite, although I knew the personal business could not be pleasant. "I'll find Papa."

To my regret Papa was home. And I left Brother Jonas in his care while I rejoined Fay. Still sitting on the steps, tugging at straps to make the skates secure, we heard voices coming through the open window.

Brother Jonas was not long driving home his point. "Brother Porter," he whined, "you know we are told in the Holy Bible to shun the very appearance of evil."

"Yes, we are," agreed Papa.

"Now, it doesn't say shun evil. It says shun the *very appearance of evil!*" he went on emphatically.

"That's right," said Papa.

"Skating rinks, we know, are dens of iniquity." He

self-consciously cleared his throat. "Do you think it's fitting for our preacher's daughter to be forever on skates?"

We bristled. "Why, the old cross-eyed son of a toad-frog!" said Fay.

"Sh-h-h, listen!" I shushed her, for Papa was answering, and on his words hung all my future joy.

"You're absolutely right, Brother Jonas," Papa said, and hope gave a dying gasp in the heart of me.

"I wish he had warts on all his fingers and all his toes," I said, tears welling up in my eyes and a lump forming in my throat.

Fay and I were ready to open the floodgates and drown ourselves in a pool of tears when Papa's voice continued, "And we do try to shun the appearance of evil. However, our little girl is frail, and the doctor has told us to use every means to see that she gets plenty of fresh air and exercise."

Hurrah for Papa! He was not giving in. He was telling the truth, to be sure; but wasn't he brilliant, thought we, to remember the truth at the right time! We hugged each other and waited to hear no more. With one long-stroke our skate wheels started rolling,

and we were off. Heigh-ho for uncensored play!

Being afflicted with poor health himself, Brother
Jonas evidently felt thereafter in the preacher's frail
daughter a kindred spirit. He took me under his wing.
"How are you feeling, honey?" he asked every time
we met. And since he was a druggist, he took it upon
himself to inform Papa of every builder-upper on the
market and, bless him, even donated to the cause—
yeast, iron tablets, tonics—the whole of which, had I
consumed, would have made of me by this time a ghost
or an Amazon.

Papa loved fun and sociability, and he provided for it
constantly. Usually it was the active type. We were
forever staging outdoor plays, with all the children of
the community taking part, and with Papa and Mother
stepping in whenever we were in need of adult coun-
sel.

Once when we had worked especially hard on a ben-
efit show—admission two cents, proceeds to go to the
Babies' Milk Fund—Papa and the Sunday-school
superintendent borrowed somewhere an army tent and
erected it for use on the vacant lot next to the church.
With such equipment we gave an inspired
performance—so inspired that it had to be twice
repeated—and we were able to contribute more of the
milk of human kindness to underprivileged babies than
we had dreamed.

No home of ours was long without a tennis court and
a croquet ground. These became gathering places for
the young people of the community. Papa made no
distinction between Judy O'Grady and the colonel's
lady. It sometimes handicapped our fun to be as demo-
cratic as he expected us to be. We had our preference
in playmates, but he would say, "A preacher's child

must show no partiality." And we were supposed to act upon that law.

Once Hugh and Cecil were criticized for not inviting two certain girls in town to play tennis. They were related to important church families, and when Papa heard the critical rumor he called the boys on the mat. "Unless you can have the Smith girls over and play with them, you'll just have to quit playing on the tennis court," was his ultimatum. Cecil and Hugh promised to ask them the very next day, and they kept the letter of the law, if not its spirit.

The next morning Cecil rode over to the Smith home on his bicycle. "Lucy, could you and Jenny play tennis with Hugh and me today?" he cordially invited.

Without consulting Jenny she responded, "We'd like to. What time?"

"Oh, say two o'clock," said Cecil, as if it were impromptu and had not been settled long ago in conspiracy with Hugh.

"We'll be there," said Lucy happily.

Two o'clock on an August afternoon in Texas! When the heat is so dreadful that no native has the desire to do anything but take off his flesh and sit in his bones.

Promptly at the appointed hour Lucy and Jenny Smith arrived, smiling and fresh-looking in crisp dotted-swiss dresses. As they had never played tennis before, Hugh patiently explained the procedure and all the rules. When they felt they were ready the game began. Fast and furiously the boys played, racing the girls from the back of the court to the net and to the back again.

When the first game was over they asked, "Do you like tennis?"

"Oh, yes," the girls forced an enthusiastic reply.

"Then let's keep on playing," Cecil urged; and back to their places on the court they went for another game of dodging tennis balls and heat waves.

Without stopping to rest, they played another and another and another. At the end of the sixth game Jenny, drenched with perspiration, her hair like string, her face the color of beet juice, edged up to Lucy, who presented an identical picture. And the boys heard what they had been so vigorously working and hopefully listening for as she exhaustedly murmured to Lucy, "We'd better go home."

"Oh, must you?" Hugh regretfully asked.

Both boys thanked them for coming and gallantly escorted them home. Subsequent invitations were given, but from that day the Smith girls showed no spark of interest in tennis—at least not on the parsonage court.

JUST as the older boys once gave urge in their play to an impromptu rodeo, so Candler drafted our cow in a little private performance. History repeats itself in the parsonage as elsewhere.

On one of those hot, lazy days of a Texas summer Mother was entertaining the Missionary Society. As usual it was our responsibility to regale the children of the members. Candler was a would-be toughie of ten, and as he and I sat on the porch steps in company with the progeny of the ladies, twiddling our thumbs and trying to think up a game, his eye lighted on Maude, our milk provider, staked out on the vacant lot.

Keeping his eye on her, with a meaningful air, he rose to his full height, gave a dust-scattering lick to the seat of his pants, and said, "C'mon, kids, follow me."

While the prayer for the heathen Chinese was being voiced in the house, the little troop outside fell into step with their dictator and followed him to the vacant lot. Maude, oblivious of her impending role in the show, continued to chew her cud and bask in cowly complacency.

"Now stand back, you kids," Red commanded, and they craw-fished to a respectful distance. Getting a running start Red shattered Maude's tranquility by running up to her and landing astride her back with a terrific thud. Then as the juvenile grandstand cheered, he dug his heels into her sides, slapped her back, and yelled, "Yip-pe-e-e!"

Mad as a hornet at such unjust handling, Maude gave a snort suggestive of a Mexican bull and headed toward the cow lot and safety. After a few leaps she suddenly came to the end of her rope with a violent halt. Before the bulging eyes of the spectators, Red bolted through the air over her head and plunged to the ground.

The ladies in the house were by that time surging through the door, "He's killed!" they screamed. "Poor child! Oh, poor child, he's killed!" They crowded about, fanning him, slapping his wrists, feeling for broken bones.

Red lay inert for a few moments, luxuriating in the lamentations; then he hopped to his feet. With a low bow and in his best grandstand voice he said, "I thank you, ladies, I thank you." And Maude, welcoming her restored serenity, resumed her chewing at the place where she had left off a few unhappy moments before.

They Came Out Singing and Dancing

MOTHER often said, "If the pulpit hadn't gotten your Father, the stage would have."

Papa loved theatricals. It has taken him quite a long time to accept moving pictures, but flesh-and-blood performances were his constant delight. He continually urged various church groups to work up a play. It was the most enjoyable way to raise money for any deficit in the church budget, and the giving of pageants was to his mind the most impressive method of observing Easter, Mother's Day, Children's Day, Thanksgiving, and Christmas.

Upon Mother's shoulders most often fell the responsibility for directing and producing the performances. It was no small task to pick out diamonds in the rough and by day-to-day practicing polish them for a glittering appearance before family and friends, and

149

at the same time keep down all feelings of envy or jealousy in the cast of characters and out of it. Nor was it a small task to build the scenery—everything from a manger for nativity plays to a cathedral for "Why the Chimes Rang." Nor was it easy with limited resources to make costumes—from shining armor for a medieval knight to ermine robes for an Oriental king. But it was exciting. And the church members as well as the family entered into the spirit of every production.

We felt especially fortunate that Mother was the director and made most of the costumes. During those weeks of preparation, into the usual down-to-earth atmosphere of the parsonage crept the glamour and romance of the stage. Strewn about Mother's room were bits of cloth in brilliant colors, cut for transforming a high-school girl into a Madonna or an adolescent boy into a Wise Man. And standing in the corner, stiff and sparkling, were angel wings—waiting to be fastened to the shoulders of some fortunate, fragile little blonde.

It was the disappointment of my church theatrical career never to have been cast as an angel. It did not occur to anybody that a dark-eyed, olive-skinned moppet could be ethereal. Heavenly figures must be delicate, Dresden-like, and, oh, so ethereal! I comforted myself, however, by donning the wings at will and prancing about the house an unappointed cherub. Unlike the visits of most angels, which are short and bright, mine lasted the better part of a week. What are a few brief moments upon the stage compared with a whole week of unrestrained wing-flapping?

ONCE, quite by accident, Mother forsook her backstage life to appear briefly before the spotlight. The Missionary Society was giving a play, one of those breakdown farces, "The Old Maid's Convention."

The ladies of the church were having the time of their lives disporting in the most ridiculous costumes they could rig up—hats with high plumes, shoes that buttoned halfway up the leg, wasp-waisted dresses, lorgnettes, and whatever else their attics could give forth. The plot, a sickly one, concerned the convening from all parts of the country of women whom life had left unwed, unhonored, and unsung. They were there to bemoan their mutual woes. From that beginning the play was mostly improvised, and every rehearsal added a few more touches.

On the night of the performance, one of the principal characters, or delegates to the convention, was ill. Mother stepped into the high-buttoned shoes and outlandish costume to take her place. None of us, nor the audience, nor Papa knew of the substitution until Mother stepped out on the stage. Usually the essence of propriety and reserve, that night she abandoned herself to the hilarity of the occasion in a way that delighted the church members, opened our eyes in unbelief, and completely floored Papa.

With head flung carelessly high she tripped perkily about the stage and at unexpected moments came shyly close to the footlights and flirted with Papa. She, the mother of eight children, was the most coy old maid at the convention. When her "special" came, she stepped to the center of the stage and lifted her voice in woeful song. Off key and with heartbreaking gestures she sang:

> Why did I let him kiss me?
>   Oh, I let him kiss me twice.
> I know that I did wrong,
>   But, oh, dear me, he seemed so-o-o nice!

And on through twelve tragic stanzas.

At home after the performance we clustered around her. For now there was a new aura about her. Our Mother could act! "We didn't know you could do that, Mother," we said. "Why don't you take part in all the plays?"

"Aren't you ashamed, Pop," said Raybon, "to have robbed the stage of such an actress?"

Papa looked over at Mother with an indulgent smile. "Sh-h-h-h" was his only comment.

CANDLER was usually drafted for a part in the church pageants, especially at Christmastime. He evaded the assignment whenever possible, for his informal nature shrank from memorizing set lines and actions.

One Christmas season when Mother had to forgo the directing, Miss Donald, who took the program in charge, cast Candler in the part of a shepherd. He refused the honor, pleading too much school work. Papa heard of it and immediately accepted the role for him. And beginning with the first rehearsal Candler obligingly said his line, "What is that great light which floods the earth? Let us go hence that we may see!" After that, in company with the other shepherds, he was to draw near to the manger and stand, propped on his shepherd's crook, for the remaining thirty minutes of the pageant without uttering a sound.

Had he been permitted to wear a more colorful costume, and sandals on his feet, he would have been less restive in his role. But he was required to garb himself in loose gray flannel, tie a rag around his head—for all the world like a housemaid—and go barefoot! That was the last straw. He was in the self-conscious age, and to have to pad up and down the aisles barefoot was ignominy too great. However,

> His not to reason why,
> His but to do or die.

And he did, although at each rehearsal there was more dying than doing.

As the time for the performance neared, only one thread of self-respect and the thought of how it would affect Papa's work kept him from running the other way. Honor stayed his feet, and a few minutes before curtain time he was among those in the dressing room, uncomfortably encased in the gray flannel, sans shoes, sans socks, sans interest. He submitted to that last touch, having an artificial beard of crepe hair stuck on his face and his eyebrows accented with a make-up pencil.

Then with faint heart, he heard the piano playing, "Silent Night, Holy Night." That was his signal to go to the entrance of the church with the other shepherds to wait their cue. They stood in the darkness of the foyer looking at the scene. In the center of the stage was a curtained stable, over which hung a bright star. Then the spotlight was directed to the back of the church for the entrance of the three shepherds. In

undertone Candler said, "C'mon, boys, we've got to
see this through," and raised his voice as he started
walking. "What is that great light which floods the
earth?" he said. "Let us go hence that we may see!"

They went hence, down the aisle and up on the platform, where they took their places to await the unfold-
ing of the rest of the pageant. The curtain was drawn,
revealing a manger with Mary seated back of it gazing
into its depths and Joseph standing proudly near her.
From the rear of the church came the unison singing of
three voices,

> We three kings of Orient are;
> Bearing gifts we traverse afar.

And singing their way the Wise Men too came upon
the scene.

All was going smoothly, shepherds quietly resting
on their crooks, Wise Men gazing with adoration at the
manger, one of them worshipfully kneeling to offer a
gift, when suddenly the seventeen-year-old Mary gave
expression to a faint giggle. The next line was hers.
"May God bless thee," she said to the Wise Man on
his knees, "for thy gift to the Child." And she ended
with a stifled laugh. The bowed Wise Man took up the
mood and joined her suppressed laughter. He looked
to Joseph for help to regain his composure, but no help
was there; for he too, with eyes directed to the floor,
was attempting to keep back his mirth. One by one the
cast succumbed, and struggled through their lines attempting to swallow the smiles which pushed their way
through the solemnity of the scene. All except Candler. His eyes too were directed to the floor, but looking down at his feet, as if in shame that the others
could so forget themselves.

As usual for a special program, the church was

crowded with visitors, and Papa fidgeted in embarrassment, as the pageant was marred by uncontrollable
giggling. Parents scattered here and there in the audience began forming the lectures which they would de-
liver to their prodigies when they got them home.
Came the final scene when the cast and audience
joined in singing "Joy to the World!"

Gathered in the living room at home later we were
discussing the pageant. "Son," Mother said to Candler appreciatively. "I'm proud of you for keeping
your face straight and not entering into that sacrile-
gious laughter. What could they have been laughing at,
anyhow?" That was the mystery which no member of
the cast had divulged at the church.

"Well, Mom," was the shamefaced reply, "I cannot
tell a lie." So saying he pulled off his shoes and socks
and placed his bare feet on the floor in view of all. On
the top of each of them, in bold black, lines, was drawn
a funny face. By certain movements of the muscles in
the feet, he could make them change expression. He
had created his additions to the cast by using the eye-
brow pencil and the rouge and powder from the
make-up box. He now looked at Papa pleadingly.
"Honest, Pop," he said, "I didn't know it would cause
such a commotion. I got so danged tired of standing
there barefoot every night doing nothing I decided to
entertain myself, and the rest of them just happened to
see it."

That was Candler's farewell biblical performance.

NOT only was Candler's formal acting career brought
to an abrupt close, but his impromptu shows also
waxed to a disastrous finish. All his life something
within his uninhibited soul was fascinated by the dis-
jointed antics of black people when they were perform-

ing. He was a regular attendant at all of their Holiness meetings, and his version of them would be served the next morning at breakfast with our oatmeal. Whenever possible he had a black playmate who was a constant source of Negro lore and dances.

During high-school days he struck up a friendship with Zeke. Unlike his prophetic namesake, Zeke moved in a way a little less than holy. He spent his happy-go-lucky days shining shoes, and between shines he spent the time, which hung heavy on his irresponsible hands, practicing the rhythms of the buzzard lope—a spineless, effortless, primitive dance.

Candler studied Zeke's movements by the hour and imitated them behind closed doors. By diligent practice he perfected the lope and would on rare occasions with his own gang give an exhibition, though the family's knowledge of it was only hearsay.

During his first year in junior college, a professor stopped him in the hall one day. "Red, I've heard among the students that you're a real actor. How about a performance on our assembly program Monday?"

"What kind of performance?" asked Candler.

"Oh, anything you like. It's all impromptu. Give us something funny."

"Okay," agreed Candler.

The professor had said, "Anything you like," and Candler liked the buzzard lope. His friends seemed to like it too.

Papa was given a special invitation to the assembly, since his son was to take part. And he was called upon to begin it with a prayer. Papa prayed. The program proceeded through varied numbers with varied content: a duet "Whispering Hope" by the Lacy sisters; a humorous reading "Maggie and Jiggs" by the school's talented expressionist; the singing of the cowboy guitarist "Oh, bury me not on the lone prairie-ee-ee." Everybody was having a fine time. Next was Candler's contribution. Nobody knew what he had chosen to do.

He went nonchalantly to the stage. "Professor White asked me the other day to perform on this program," he said. "I will now perform."

He walked to the far end of the platform and paused. Rubbing his hand over his face, he left it with a fixed, vacant expression. Then he gave his trousers a lazy hitch at the waist in back and in front, raising the cuffs to a high-water mark, and went into his speciality. Slowly he began to glide across the stage in a silent, effortless movement, like a giant earthworm which had raised itself to a vertical position. By the time he was across the stage and revolving to complete the circle, his schoolmates were convulsed at the boneless body, dumbly undulating before their eyes. Papa had no idea that his son could do such a stunt, and having a keen sense of humor, he too was bending toward his knees in unrestrained laughter. There was only one thing he regretted—Mother was missing it.

He had to leave immediately after Candler's number

to meet another engagement. At home, later in the day, he said, "Candler has been holding out on us. Have him do his act for you when he gets here."

When the buzzard loper reached home that afternoon, however, he entered the house with slow steps.

"Pop " he moaned, "I guess I'll be Mother's home companion from now on. I'm expelled!"

"Expelled?" said Papa in unbelief. "What on earth have you been doing?"

"According to some of the faculty members," he said, "I did a wicked, heathenish dance on the assembly program this morning. I will now be dropped from the roll."

Papa's program for the next day was automatically rearranged. He went into a long conference with the school president and faculty members. When he emerged his youngest—the pagan dancer—was reinstated in school.

Years later, after all of us were away from home, we were having a family get-together in a town to which Papa had just been assigned as pastor of the Methodist church. Candler's sinful farewell to acting and Papa's innocent enjoyment of it were being recalled. A sister-in-law, new in the family, said, "Do you remember the buzzard lope, Candler? Please do it for us." The rest of us joined in the urging, and Candler rose to give a command performance. He shifted his facial expression to neutral, hitched his trousers, and started moving. Like the other audience, we were convulsed.

Papa, passing through the brightly lighted living room at that particular moment, paused to laugh with us—until he made a heartsinking observation. "Children!" he said in stricken tone above the laughter. "Sh-h-h-h, children—*the shades are up!*"

Peace on Earth

Oh, what mean those voices singing?
Oh, what mean those bells a-ringing
All through the night?

The bells at Christmastide! What sheer joy floods
the heart of every adult when they resound through
memory, ringing back the magic of childhood and an
old-fashioned Christmas. In our childhood we not only
kept Christmas; we made Christmas. We made our
gifts, we made the wrappings, we made the tree trimmings, and we made our entertainment. How good it
was to make Christmas.

Christmas shopping was comparatively unknown,

but creating presents filled the weeks preceding the holiday with exciting secrecy.

"I'm making something for you that is this high and about so-o-o wide," one of the boys would say, weeks before Christmas, measuring dimensions in the air.

"Is it a doll bed?" I would ask.

"No."

"A shelf for my books?"

"No."

"Oh, I know now—I know," hoping by such a bluff to get a clue.

"Oh, no you don't; and you needn't keep guessing, 'cause it's nothing you ever saw or heard of before."

Curiosity would be all-consuming, but to no avail. And on Christmas Eve, from the church tree would be handed down, in all probability, the long-dreamed-of doll bed.

Bright woolen yarns for knitting mittens and scarves, cloth for making new garments, wood for fashioning toys to delight the heart of a child were brought home weeks ahead; and moments of work were snatched in secret each day for the making of presents. For each of us there were nine gifts to make for the family alone—before planning for friends.

But the giving of gifts and the hanging of stockings for Santa constituted only a small part of our celebration of Christmas.

Who more than a minister's child has an opportunity to learn the true meaning of Christmas? For at that season, more than any other, the church has a mission in bringing joy to the world. There are the poor of the community to remember with gifts and food, the shut-ins to be serenaded with carols of "Holy Night," and people of all faiths and of no faith coming to services to honor and commemorate the birthday of the Christ. Christmas is a high joy to be shared by the whole world!

A TREE at home was unheard of in our childhood. A giant one was always erected in the church for the enjoyment of all. Only the noblest cedar in the forest was worthy to be called a Christmas tree. On the Monday before Christmas several stewards would meet at the church. They would move the piano and the pulpit from the rostrum, unscrew from their stands all the choir seats, and move them down among the pews.

Then they would go into the woods, select a tree, and bring it to the church. It would be placed in the center of the platform and nailed down, and its top would touch the ceiling.

When the lordly tree had been transplanted it was time for the trimming sessions. Each department of the Sunday school created a part of the decorations; and every child, by being permitted to string popcorn or paste bright-colored paper rings together and place them on the tree, was made to feel that it was his very own. A certain hour was designated for each group to meet and add its touch. The sky was the limit on ingenious trimmings, and the tree was large enough to give outlet for combined creative effort.

Living next door to the church had its compensations during the holiday season. I attended each trimming. So afraid was I that something would go on the tree without my observance that I did not bother to go by the house on the way home from school, but raced, red scarf flying in the wind, straight to the church each afternoon.

''But you must come by the house and let me know

you are home from school!'' Mother would say.

"Oh, Mother, I just can't!'' I would tell her. "Miss Lacy said she specially needed me to help her today. And besides, I might be late to the 'practice.' ''

The "practice" was the all-important rehearsal for the Christmas program. Special programs were given throughout the week before Christmas, but the pinnacle hour was the program and tree at the church on Christmas Eve.

While some members of the family were reluctant to take part in the programs, others were ready at the drop of a hat. And I was one. Christmas would not have been Christmas without a part on the program. My earliest recollection is of walking to the platform, standing in front of a huge, candlelit tree, and reciting:

> Little Jesus, wast Thou shy
> Once, and just as small as I?
> And what did it feel like to be
> Out of heaven, and just like me?

The next year the program called for a little-girl soloist. Standing in semidarkness, looking at a tin-foil star suspended on a wire, which to me was twinkling with reality, I lifted my voice to sing:

> Little star, away up yonder,
>   Tell me were you shining then?
> Did you hear the angels singing,
>   "Peace on earth, good will to men"?

After each program, lighted only by the candles on the tree, the audience would softly sing "O Little Town of Bethlehem" and "Hark! the Herald Angels Sing," ending with "Silent Night, Holy Night." Time does not erase the poignant sacredness of those moments.

THE programs were always given in front of the massive tree, which was smiling and sagging with gay packages for everybody in the church. For it was the custom that all gifts be brought to the church tree—for family, for friends, for the poor. The tree was almost obscured with everything from cedar chests to handkerchiefs, from rocking chairs to baseball bats, from bicycles to dolls—not to mention a sack of fruit and nuts for every person present, a gift from the Sunday school. The overflow was stacked under the tree, but not till all tying space was gone. Everybody saw what everybody got and who gave what to whom.

The most exciting moment was that one immediately after the close of the program when we waited breathlessly for the arrival of Santa Claus. He was always obligingly prompt. We had no opportunity of seeing Santa in the stores before Christmas. The only place he was ever to be seen was at the church on Christmas Eve.

Exactly on time outside the church would come a prancing of hoof and, "Whoa, Donner and Blitzen! There, Dancer! Now, Prancer!" as Santa would alight from his sleigh. Delighted squeals emanated from various spots over the audience. Little faces were hidden on their mothers' shoulders; for the excitement of seeing the jovial presence, with masked features like to no human being, was almost too much. Joy at his coming and fear of his reality overflowed the hearts of the children. The door would open, and through it would burst a jolly, laughing Santa, with red suit, high black

boots, and bells, bells, bells jingling as he walked.
Down the aisle he would come, stamping the snow
from his boots and blowing warmth into his cold
hands. "Hello, everybody!" he would shout. "I made
it, didn't I?" And, his eye catching the eye of some
child on the aisle, he would pause. "Well, well, here's
Johnny Green! Have you been a good boy?" Santa
knew our names!

Before my courage was developed to the point of
close contact with Santa I begged Mother on Christmas Eve, "Please, promise that we won't sit next to
the aisle!" It was frenzied joy to see Santa Claus, but
much more comfortable at a slight distance than too
near his overpowering presence.

After shaking hands here and there up the aisle,
Santa would go to the tree for that glorious ceremony
of distributing gifts. Then the supreme elation of getting and opening presents—and showing them all
around—with the chant of Santa's voice going on.
"Gladys Short!" he would call, waving over his head a
brightly colored package. "Are you here, Gladys?
Now here's something for Carol Roundtree. Where are
you, Carol?" One must sit forward on the edge of the
bench; for her name might be called and she wouldn't
hear it! On and on it went till near midnight—the calling of names, distributing presents—and the smallest
children stayed wide awake.

Santa would take an occasional rest and let his
helpers carry on. The more courageous children could
then slip up to the platform, where he sat near the tree,
and talk in low tones with him.

IT was at the church tree that I learned the truth about
Santa Claus. Corpulent old Brother Mahoney, who sat
in the same corner of the church every Sunday, had,

besides a surplus of *Amens,* a chronic sniffle. It was always a source of interest to me, because it was so unusual—really four sniffles in one. When Papa was preaching over my head or repeating a sermon I had heard, I would amuse myself by listening and counting time to Brother Mahoney's sniffles. They were rhythmical: one long sniff—a pause of two counts—then three staccato sniffs—one long sniff—pause—count one, two, three shorts—and in a few minutes, repeat! He never failed to come in on the right beat. He never failed to make the same number of sniffs.

During one of those intimate little talks with Santa near the tree one Christmas Eve, all at once I heard from Santa's nostrils a hauntingly familiar sniff! "H'mm," thought I, but wholly without suspicion, "sounds kinda like Brother Mahoney."

"Kinda?" whispered reason arguing with innocence. "You mean *just* like!" And a sickening chill ran down my spine. I stepped aside to let someone else talk to him. "I'll count," said I to myself, "and then I'll know." So I counted. One long sniff—pause—one, two,—oh, bitter truth! there followed one after the other three staccato sniffs. Blinded with tears I found my way to Mother and hid my face on her shoulder in

painful disillusionment. At home that night I tearfully demanded an explanation. I went to bed somewhat comforted after Mother's words, "Anybody who loves children and spreads joy at Christmas can be Santa," she said. "You can be. How would you like to be Santa to Candler and the others and fill their stockings?" And I was waked at the proper time to share in the filling of the stockings, for everybody's stocking hung on the mantel every year that he was home.

THE celebration at the church could have its pathos as well as its joy. Clear in my memory is the time when one of my little schoolmates sat next to me watching breathlessly the presents being handed down from the tree and listening for her name to be called. Her father was reputed to be the wealthiest and stingiest man in town, and at Christmastime he was an old Scrooge. There were several children in the family. The older ones did not come to the tree, perhaps because they knew how embarrassing it could be. And the mother, a chronic invalid, could not be there. But little Penelope, with faith and confidence, came. For two hours of constant name calling her hopes went up and down. True, she had a sack of fruit and nuts passed around by Santa's helpers, and she even had a handkerchief that someone had dropped as a surprise into her lap; but her name had not been called. Toward the end, when only a few scattered packages remained on the tree, I could stand the look on her face no longer. I worked my way to Mother and whispered the story. "It hasn't been called once, Mother," I told her, "and she's just about to cry!"

"We won't let her be disappointed," said Mother. She took a small bottle of perfume, which I had tied on the tree for her, carefully rewrapped it, and wrote across the wrapping "Penelope Warren." Candler was sent with it unobtrusively up to the tree, with directions to call Santa's attention to it. Just as hope had died within the little girl's heart, Santa Claus called out in a loud important voice, "Penelope Warren."

She danced up and down with joy. "He did call it! He did call it!" she cried. "I did get a present." What mattered the contents of the box when before everybody, in impressive tone, her name had been called!

OTHER children came precariously near to disillusionment on one Christmas Eve—through the fault of Santa Claus himself. A heavy-set, imposing gentleman was chosen to play the role. He was selected for more than one reason: he looked the part, and also he was a new member of the church. If given the responsibility of performing an important part in its program, he would more nearly feel that he "belonged." During the previous summer Brother Damon had been converted in a revial meeting and rescued from the fiery furnace. Fat as a porpoise, jolly as a sailor, he made a perfect Santa, and he reveled in his stellar role.

The tree was lighted after the manner of the day, with candles. In his hilarity as he bent towards the audience calling out, "Whose present is this? Let me see," Santa backed up too near a candle. The cotton batting on the midriff of his suit caught fire. Two men sitting on the front pew discovered the catastrophe before Santa and were making their way toward him to extinguish the blaze when Santa, feeling the warmth, was himself struck with the realization of what had happened.

Brother Damon had renounced the ways of the

world only that summer, be it remembered, and some of its lingo came automatically to his lips in time of stress. "————!" he yelled. "Help me out of this thing, somebody! Help me out of this thing!"

The pianist fortunately was quick-witted enough to thunder out some Christmas music, while some of the men whisked the disgruntled Santa out through the back vestibule. Papa had to save the day and the illusions of the young. He peered through the door into the vestibule. "I'll tell them, Santa," he said and came to the center of the platform. "He says to tell all you boys and girls that he has another coat in his pack and that he has to hurry on now or he won't make it around to your houses to fill your stockings." The congregation sang the customary closing hymn, "Joy to the World!" and we went home to await a happier visit from Santa Claus.

SANTA's head must have whirled when he dropped through our chimney to be faced with ten stockings of varying lengths hanging in an expectant line across the mantel. He always placed a silver coin deep within the toe of each and topped it off with a generous supply of nuts, fruit, and peppermint candy. Oranges were a

Christmas delight, and if we had been especially good he left two in our stocking. Since the larger presents were given at the church, only the small remembrances and joke gifts were placed in our stockings.

On Christmas morning Papa had no chance to stand in the hall giving his familiar "come crawling" call, for we were crowding the living room. "Merry Christmas, Mother! Merry Christmas, Papa! Merry Christmas, everybody!" Raybon at the piano would be playing "Jingle Bells," while around the room we went, showing our gifts, playing with our toys, singing snatches of the song.

If the parsonage kept open house on other days, it kept opener house on Christmas Day. Mother would have prepared mince pies, dressing and cranberries, and fruit cakes in plenty. And just as fowl was provided for our table on Sunday, on Christmas some member was sure to present his pastor with a huge turkey. No restrictions were made on the number of guests we might invite to dinner or call during the day. And God blessed us every one.

Although time has altered customs, and no longer do most churches plan a service for Christmas Eve, still on the night before Christmas I find my heart and my steps ever turning toward a church, for somehow within the holy hush of the house of God I can more clearly hear the angels singing, "On earth peace, good will toward men."

Many Waters Cannot Quench Love

"DADDY, Daddy, Daddy!" A voice strangely like, yet strangely unlike, Raybon's eighteen-year-old tenor came from the kitchen. Since none of us ever addressed Papa that informally my ears refused to believe what they heard, and as I curiously stepped to the kitchen door my eyes refused to believe what they saw. On the ironing board was a half-ironed shirt. Back of it stood Raybon, lifting pleading arms and coy eyes into the thin air above his head as his voice in baby tones begged, "Take me, Daddy, take me!" Then he turned to the other side and impishly demanded, "No, Daddy, take me!" And last to the center, tearfully whining, "Me, Daddy, Me!"

Alarmed lest his brain had snapped, I tried to speak to Mother, who was busy at the stove back of him, but she raised a silencing finger as the scene continued. There was a long pause, during which Raybon's expression indicated that baby feet were pattering through his imagination, and once more a baby voice pleaded, "Daddy, Daddy, Daddy!" Then the visionary dropped to a stool, rested his elbows on the ironing board and his chin in his hands. "Oh, Mother," he sighed. "I just can't wait till I hear my babies calling me Daddy."

Relieved that he was sane, but utterly disgusted, I started again to speak, and once more came Mother's silencing motion. Never by word or look would she dispel the dream of another or allow us to. "Mother," Raybon dreamily continued, "how do you know when you are really in love?"

Bored with the conversation, I went through the kitchen and out the back door, but Mother's reply came to my ears. "Don't even think of marrying, until down deep you absolutely know that you can't live without her."

Her words have echoed down the years and have penetrated for me many surface relationships "until down deep you absolutely know you can't live without him."

During our ministerial wanderings, six of us have found, in one town or another, a fireside companion for future years. Before shooting the fatal arrow, however, Cupid spent many an arduous hour aiming and retrieving practice darts.

A RHYMIST once wrote:

> Everywhere I look I see—
> Fact or fiction, life or play,

Still the little game of Three:
B and C in love with A.

Cecil and Raybon were ever enamored of the same
girl. They were hardly out of pinafores, when a love
arrow split in mid-air and struck with equal force each
of their little-boy hearts.

Once a friend of Mother's had come to spend the
afternoon, bringing her curly-haired four-year-old
daughter. At first sight the two boys became her slaves
and vied all afternoon for her exclusive attention.
When the afternoon was over and good-byes were
being said at the buggy, it was discovered that little
Cleopatra's pink sunbonnet had been forgotten. An-
tony and Caesar, living again in Raybon and Cecil,
rushed to get the sacred garment. They emerged from
the house each tugging at a string, almost tearing the
bonnet. By unspoken agreement, they tossed it to the
ground and engaged in a fierce duel with fists as
weapons. While the battle raged, Mother retrieved the
bonnet, and the child's mother tied it in place. As they
drove away, her highness under the pink sunbonnet
smiled sweetly and waved two hands at two red-faced
little boys, who were alternately stuffing in shirttails
and waving, each confident that in her heart he was
really the favored one.

As Mother turned from her good-bye she was
alarmed to see that Cecil was attempting to hide a deep
gash over his right temple, cut by a sharp rock during
the combat. Raybon was sent for the doctor, but his
swift arrival was to no avail. Cecil steadfastly refused
to let him take stitches in the wound, turning a deaf ear
even to the bribe of a bantam hen. To this day he bears
a scar from that battle.

As time wore on the scar became faint, but not the rivalry. While they were in college, a girl who had granted both of them dates the year before wrote to Cecil, delighting him with the news that she would arrive by train the following Friday night to grace the city for a weekend, and that she would be pleased if he would meet her. Raybon learned by accident, through mutual friends, of her coming. He sweetly relinquished all claim to the family car for the evening, borrowed a friend's car, dressed to the hilt, and rushed to the station. As he mounted the steps two at a time, joy died within him at discerning a familiar figure at the top of the stairs.

There was no opportunity for a mutual "What are you doing here?" since the charming guest was at that moment coming into view. Raybon grabbed her bag and started down the stairs, while Cecil fell in step beside her, chatting gaily. As they passed through the street door, he guided her to the family car, parked in opposite direction to Raybon's borrowed one. Raybon hurried toward his car with the bag, but when the divergence of ways was discovered, the worm carrying the bag turned. Wheeling about, he dropped it to the middle of the sidewalk and left it there, then quickened his step to overtake the two. Flinging peevishly by he growled into Cecil's ear, "If you're going to walk with her, you may also carry her bag!"

Finding balm for his bruised heart kept Raybon out later than usual that night, and Cecil was pulling the sheet over him, when he heard Raybon's step making the customary rounds of the bedrooms, before coming to the room which the two of them shared with Hugh and Edd. Raybon's affection flowed not only to the fair sex but also to his family, and as long as he lived at

home, he nightly bent over each bed and placed a kiss
on the forehead of Papa, Mother, brothers, and sisters.
It had long irked Cecil to be kissed by his affectionate
brother, and on this particular night, he relished it less
than ever. He quickly turned in bed, placing his head
at the foot; and when Raybon, in darkness, bent tenderly over the pillow his kiss was planted not on a
forehead but upon one of Cecil's wiggling feet.

THE room which the four older boys shared was to me
the choice one in the house. It was the "gallery."
Everywhere were faces of gals, gals, gals—adorning
the walls, the bureau, and the study table.

I used to pick a time when I was sure none of the
four would be bursting into the room, and roam
through the gallery to study the portraits. Why was
Edd so smitten with Felice? I would ask myself. Was it
the toss of her head? The way she held her mouth? The
sparkle of her eye? Taking Felice from the study table
to the bureau I would stand her near the mirror. Then
with elbow on the bureau, propping my chin on my
hand, I would lean close to her face, and with soul-
searching scrutiny, try to fathom the mystery. When I
arrived at the solution, I would turn to the mirror and
for the next thirty minutes completely lose myself in
Felice-like posing—and in making up words to go with
the gestures.

It was a constant source of interest to see which girls
stayed longest in the running, for every so often some
photograph would be placed in the bureau drawer
while a newer, brighter flame would take its place.
Knowing nothing of the psychology of adolescent
boys, I did not like this off-with-the-old-and-on-with-

the-new policy. Just as I was feeling a warm kinship with some sweet-looking girl—though I might never have seen her—she would be relegated to the drawer and some bold flapper put in her place.

However, it taught me a lesson—not to give my photograph to a boy, unless I was willing eventually to be committed to a bureau drawer. And what woman is?

Cecil was the most reticent of the boys, and he laid less claim than the others to photography space. And, too, his circle was interdenominational, and Papa preferred Methodist girls. Cecil's art collection, always large, was housed in a private vault at the church. The pulpit has a cupboard effect with a door on the back side. Space inside was ordinarily used for storing old hymnbooks or Sunday-school papers. There, in seclusion, Cecil's portrait heartthrobs lived in amity, and at any overwhelmingly lonely moment, he could slip into the church and in its solitude gaze upon a beloved face.

But one Sunday the private gallery was inadvertently opened to the public. In the midst of an enthusiastic sermon, Papa began to quote a hymn which he could not finish:

> Soldiers of Christ, arise,
> And put your armor on . . . .

Hurriedly, he opened the little door of the pulpit and fumbled about in the recess for a hymnbook. After an embarrassing pause, he succeeded in bringing one out, but not the hymnbook alone. With it came a bevy of pictures of smiling girls, fluttering happily to the less-crowded confines of the rostrum, flagrantly waving before the amused eyes of choir members such inscrip-

`tions as TO CECIL, WITH ALL MY LOVE—I LOVE
YOU—FOREVER YOURS.

HUGH suffered no such humiliating experiences, since
he went with one girl at a time and gave her his undivided attention. It was so undivided that Papa's dead-
line of eleven o'clock for getting home was repeatedly
violated. As scoldings and warnings did no good, Papa
had to devise another method for inducing obedience.

One midnight, when the sleeping household still
lacked Hugh, Papa stripped a bed of its top sheet and
tiptoed out of the house. He went to a bridge over
which Hugh's homeward trek would bring him. There
in the shadow he draped the sheet about him and concealed his ghostly self in anticipation of Hugh's step, It
came soon, a brisk trot. As it neared the bridge, the
phantom figure rose from out of the shadow into the
moonlight. When Hugh's terrified eyes saw the vision,
his trot changed to a gallop. His breath came hard as
the sinister figure moved, then started in pursuit. Step
for step, gallop for gallop, down the road they went,

Hugh's ears warning him every step that with the next one he would be clutched in a ghostly embrace. But somehow he managed to stay one step ahead. Nearing home and faint with exhaustion he moaned, "Oh, Papa, Papa, is it you? I think it's you; but please, Papa, tell me it's you." Papa did not reassure him until years later. But at eleven o'clock the next night and each night thereafter, Hugh was among those present and accounted for.

Once a later girl of Hugh's, whom he had met during a summer revival meeting as student-preacher, became fearful that his attention was divided. He had merely lost interest—since an object in possession seldom retains the charm that it had in pursuit—and it had been weeks since he had written to her. She sent a telegram to him asking, "Why don't you write?" Hugh was head over heels in school work and truthfully wired back, "I am married to my Alma Mater." That seemed to settle the matter.

But two weeks later a package arrived for him. We crowded about the dinner table, as he opened the package, to see what could prompt a gift on no special occasion. As the last fold of paper was removed and the lid on the box was raised, we saw shining with beauty a set of six silver teaspoons—and with them a card from the girl of the telegram: BEST WISHES TO YOU AND ALMA FOR YOUR HAPPINESS!

MOST of our love affairs involved the family. We have often wondered how an only child carries on the necessary steps of courtship. Who acts as courier for love notes, if not a younger brother? Who is the mediator in a lovers' quarrel? And who stands sentinel near the place of rendezvous in case a parent should call?

When one of Edd's high-school love affairs had reached the stage of needing daily fuel, leaving home every day could have been a problem, except for our motto ONE FOR ALL AND ALL FOR ONE. Three of the other boys rallied around him, and life held no further complications.

Every afternoon an hour before suppertime, Candler would make it a point to play in our front yard, Gil would stroll a block away and play with a friend, while a block and a half further on, Raybon would walk a beat. And Edd would sit with his sweetheart on her front doorstep. All agreed that each would move within that radius, until Papa's whistle should sound through the air. Then Candler would pick it up, relay it to Gil, who would echo it to Raybon, who would warn Edd that the rendezvous must end. Edd would bear the sweet sorrow of parting and join Raybon, the two would catch up with Gil, and within a few minutes all would be trooping into the house for supper.

When Papa wished an audience with one of his children, he did not call that one by name. He would simply step to the back door and emit a whistle like unto no other whistle, and in response children would scurry from all directions.

WHISTLE relaying was only one mode of furthering the cause of love for each other. There was also tree sitting. Sister admits that she would never have snared her breadwinner, Harry, whom she first courted in high school, had not Gil, Candler, and I been always stationed in a treetop to announce his coming. Between that and his arrival, she could change her dress or powder her nose. When the two of them would have a clandestine meeting—Papa thought Sister too young for dates—we could see the approach of any tattletale and sound an alarm. From our exalted position we saw all, heard all, and, knew all. To keep us from telling cost Sister and her sweetheart many an anxious moment, and many a piece of silver.

For them there was no escape, for between the time of school's closing and the time for school's opening we literally lived in the trees. We would nail planks to the limbs and carry up books, pillows, toys, bottles of water, and fruit. Mother would fix our lunch in a basket and tie it to the long rope left dangling from the tree for that purpose. We would ascend to our arboreal penthouses the first thing every morning and descend to the mundane world at night only in time to go to bed. At those dizzy heights we played house and store, read to each other, wrote poems, and carried on a conversation with everybody who passed under the tree on his way uptown. Quite without intending to do so, we gave Mother day after day of peace without her three youngest children underfoot.

At the age of twelve, Gil went so thoroughly native as to establish a love nest for his best girl in a separate tree from ours. He chose the tallest, prettiest tree in the yard. The money he earned delivering groceries on Saturday afternoon provided candy and soda pop for their ménage during the week. With such refreshments in view, Candler and I would often slide down from our tree and climb up theirs for a visit. But when we stayed overlong and ate overmuch for customary politeness, Gil would become gruff. "Go home! Sit in your own tree!"

After we were grown, tree sitting became for one

season a fad throughout the country. Marathon sittings were being achieved in this town and that. Mother and Papa lived at the time in the town where the world's champion tree sitter sat his way to fame. For weeks curiosity seekers came from far and near to walk around the tree, to peer up into its branches at the fifteen-year-old boy comfortably lodged there, and to read the signs sticking up from the ground: MEALS FROM GUY'S CAFE—THE TREE SITTER EATS DANIEL'S ICE CREAM—MILK PROVIDED BY BEECHAM'S DAIRY.

Week after week the boy sat, eating Guy's meals and drinking Beecham's milk. Papa called him Zachaeus. "Only the coming of the Lord will bring him down," he said. During the steady excitement attendant upon such a celebrated happening, Mother went about her daily tasks as usual, and not once did she walk around the corner to see the phenomenon.

One day a neighbor rushed in. "Mrs. Porter," her words stumbled over each other in excitement, "our tree sitter has won the world's championship! In ten minutes he will be coming down. Aren't you going to see him now?"

Mother, unimpressed, smiled at her. "Why should I?" she asked. "I have the *original* tree sitter in my own family. Only," she laconically added, "I wasn't farsighted enough to put out a sign."

IT was during that tree-sitting span of years that I first fell desperately in love. I had given my heart away in the first grade, again in the second, and once more in the third—but always with the feeling that it was only for a time. Now in the mature state of being nine years old and approaching the fifth grade, I felt safe in giving my heart for keeps.

But the object of my affection did not take to tree sitting. It was too tame. "I like to be high," he said, "but I like to be in an airplane going fast."

Even the word *airplane* was a recent addition to our vocabulary, and I had never actually laid eyes on one. I wanted to ask Jack if he had ever been up in one, but he talked so positively of the sensation that the question seemed superfluous. Such high-sounding talk swept me completely off my feet. Every day he would come strolling by and call up to me. Closing my book, I would come down from my tree to sit with him on the church steps, while he talked of being an aviator.

One day as he talked, the glory shone round him so brightly I had to move a foot away in sheer awe. "Dad's going to give me an airplane when I graduate from high school," he said, trying to appear casual, "and the very next day I'm going to fly to Mars!"

After the respectful silence due such a stupendous announcement, I weakly asked, "Could you really do that?"

"Of course! Just because nobody has is no sign I can't."

"Why don't you just fly across the ocean?" I suggested.

His reply reeked with disgust. "Shoot a monkey! If that's not just like a girl! Who wants to fly across the ocean? We *know* what's over *there!*"

When school opened and we walked to and from classes together, he continued to talk of flying to Mars. And I listened with the cold realization that, after that flight, I should never see him again but would eke out my days in loneliness.

One day, however, the whole world changed! Walking leisurely along, Jack kicked a rock aimlessly from the sidewalk. "Alyene," he said, "I've got to fly to Mars, but I don't want to leave you. Could—could you marry me—and maybe we could go there on our honeymoon?"

A honeymoon to Mars! Lucky me! Who better than I can know Anne Lindbergh's thrill when she was planning that first flight with the Lone Eagle? Needless to say, I accepted his proposal before he finished the voicing of it. And thereafter in school, back of our books, across the room our eyes would meet while Jack, suggesting an airplane with his right hand, would make it zoom upward as high as it could without going over the top of his geography.

One day we became afire with eagerness, when the teacher brought up for discussion the subject of Mars. No more responsive students could be found anywhere than we two as she talked, and when the bell rang, history was made in the annals of schooldom by the audible groaning of two children.

As we broke line on the school steps, Jack hurried to me. "Let's go back in and tell Miss Boutwell about our honeymoon," he whispered.

We found her alone in the room straightening her desk. Timidly we approached her, one on either side. "Miss Boutwell," I said in meaningful tone, "we have a secret to tell you."

"A secret?" she said, and circled an arm around each of us. "What could it be?"

"You'd never guess in a hundred years," Jack said, "so I'll tell you." He came close to her ear and in a loud whisper announced, "We are going to get married and fly to Mars!"

Be it said to her glorious credit, at such startling

news Miss Boutwell did not bat an eye. ''How wonderful!'' she exclaimed as she stepped into our secret, and for several minutes the three of us discussed the venture in all seriousness, until at length she sent us on our way rejoicing. There was a teacher!—taking with delicate understanding the dream of two eager youngsters, holding it tenderly for a moment, and handing it back to them bright and shining. Blessings on her! Nor did she ever betray our confidence to our parents.

As MOTHER and Papa were having to bear at that time the home reactions of six other love affairs in various stages, it was well that mine did not come to their notice.

Sister's case was unquestionably the most obtrusive. Its exact temperature was never a secret, for her sweetheart owned a trumpet with which he expressed his feeling. Music was the food of love, and he played on. If there had been a quarrel, he would stand on his porch and lift the trumpet to his lips, and when the plaintive strains of ''I'm Sorry I Made You Cry'' were wafted through our window to hover over the supper table, Sister would burst into tears and have to be excused from the room. If all was well between them, he would play, for all the town to hear, "I Love You Truly." Throughout the course of their love both family and neighbors were kept musically informed regarding its progress.

Mother and Father bore up under the strain of that and all other pupply loves and real romances, to find themselves eventually with only one child at home— Candler, who was still in school. Having no whistle relayers or tree sitters to help his romances placed him in difficulty. Necessity became the mother of invention. Candler's bedroom was upstairs, and there, under the pretense of studying, he would retire every school evening to carry on a voluminous correspondence with the girls whom he was allowed to date only on weekends. Before climbing the stairs, Candler always bestowed a goodnight kiss upon the cheek of both parents. But later in the evening, Papa would ascend to give his baby boy a tuck-in kiss.

For weeks Mother had puzzled over the invariable faint tinkling of a bell, which came to her ears every night at the same time she heard Papa's step on the stairway. One morning she questioned Candler, "Son, do you hear a bell ringing somewhere every night?"

"Yes'm I do," he confessed with a grin. "That's my Papa alarm."

"Your Papa alarm?" she asked.

"Yes'm. You see, Pop got there one night and was knocking on the door before I could get my letter out of sight, so I fixed up a little signal to keep that from happening again."

The Papa alarm consisted of a tiny bell, with cord

attached, suspended over Candler's desk. The cord was taut and ran under the door into the hall, where, by the aid of thumbtacks, it ran along the stairway wall. To the cord was tied a dark string, and to the string a black thread. The thread was stretched tightly across the second step. Without being conscious of it Papa would walk through the thread and break it. This would release the string, which held the cord, which held the bell, and would cause this last to fall with a warning jingle on Candler's desk. By the time Papa was at the door the letter would be in the drawer and schoolbooks upon the desk. One of the older boys might have been punished for such a plot, but with the baby it was different. Papa is still laughing over Candler's inventive ways.

As EACH child discovered the one whom down deep he knew he couldn't live without, Papa would somewhat tearfully take his place to perform the marriage ceremony. We were all baptized by bishops, but we were married by Papa. The ceremonies varied from small home weddings to formal church ones, and every one was performed in a different town. Hugh's was hard, since it was first. But then, for one reason or another, it was with reluctance that each was given up—Sister because she was the oldest girl, and on and on.

As he spoke the rites at each ceremony, Papa's face became pale, and emotion seethed within him. He was probably most visibly affected when it came the hour for saying the marriage ceremony for Candler, the baby. Candler had sighed to many, though he loved but one, and he could not wait to finish college to claim her as his bride. He had no work, no prospect of any, but the wedding went on as planned, and in the presence of the two families.

A few minutes before the ceremony, Mother discovered Candler in the back bedroom busily engaged in tying into a bundle on a stick, hobo style, three shirts, a tie, and some socks.

"What are you doing, son?" she asked.

"Well, Mom," he said, "this is for when I say, 'With all my worldly goods I thee endow.' "

During the ceremony, Gil's eight-year-old son, who had slipped into witness this bedroom scene, sat by Mother, quiet and subdued by the solemnity of the occasion. He made no move during the rites, until Candler spoke those words about "worldly goods." Then G.R. leaned toward Mother with a joke he had heard on the radio—"There goes his football sweater." His intended whisper filled the room. Even Papa had to laugh.

The Memory Is Blessed

HUGH'S marriage marked the end of a significant period in our family life—the years when all eight of us children were together in our parsonage home. As Candler was only six when Hugh left, they were all too few. Though each of us feels a share in what came before he was born and after he went out into the world, we cherish the memory of those years of love and growth we spent all together.

If but one moment of them we could hold in our hands forever, it would be the Silver Wedding Anniversary, when Papa and Mother reenacted their mar-

riage ceremony with the eight of us as their wedding
party.

More than a hundred friends came to share our happiness. As they arrived Edd, always dignified, and Gil,
our "Hero of Information," ushered them to their
places.

When all was in readiness, Janette took her place at
the piano, as she had done for countless other weddings, and played Schubert's "Serenade." Then Cecil
read lines from Robert Browning:

> Grow old along with me!
> The best is yet to be,
> The last of life, for which the first was made. . . .

The voice was Cecil's voice, but the words were as if
Mother herself spoke them, for had she not coached
Cecil in the interpretation for weeks? As Janette began
a musical prelude, I stepped forward to recite James
Whitcomb Riley's much-loved poem "An Old
Sweetheart of Mine." Attired in a rustling, full-skirted
taffeta dress to fill the dream of any child and to deflate
the pocketbook of any preacher, I rose to the height of
ten-year-old solemnity. Raybon followed. Standing
near the piano he sang:

> Ah, Love, 'tis something to feel your kind hand;
> Ah, yes, 'tis something by your side to stand. . . .

Then came the wedding march. Hugh, twenty-three
and already a full-fledged minister, walked up to take
his place at the altar, banked with pink gladioli and
fern. Candler sedately marched forward with a white
satin pillow bearing the ring, the same gold band with

which Papa and Mother had sealed their vows a quarter century before.

Mother entered on Papa's arm, and together they stood at the altar facing Hugh. Papa looked proudly down at his ''bride,'' who was gowned in soft gray chiffon over shell pink. Her hair was delicately gray now, and her cameo beauty was luminous in the candlelight.

''Edwin, wilt thou have this woman to thy wedded wife . . .?''

''I will,'' Papa tenderly responded.

Turning to Mother, Hugh asked the corresponding question, and lifting sweetly companionable eyes to Papa, she replied, ''I will.''

After the final *Amen* Hugh remained in his place and, striking the same dignified air that Papa always used for his first sermon in a new place, spoke briefly to our friends:

''It has been said that we always seem young to those who are older and old to those who are younger. Twenty-five years seem a long time to me, since that is more years than I have lived. But we think of our parents as still young, because they have heard the challenge of the great educator who said, 'Come, let us live *with* our children.' Some parents live for their children, but ours are living with us. They have always entered into our play, our work, our study. And so we grow together.

''We have had our problems and heartaches, as do all families. But, as the oldest, I speak for the others in saying that our parsonage life is a happy one. We would not exchange it for the wealth of kings.''

IT was only a few months afterward that Hugh married, and in too-rapid succession others began to go.

And then one day Mother characteristically stepped out ahead upon an unfamiliar path. Years of living so near the heart of life had weakened her own heart. But she continued to drink deeply and joyously of experience, until that day when in the midst of it, serenely as she had lived, she stepped into the greater silence.

And as she walks in splendor, the valiant heart of her in eight younger hearts beats on. Her love is in our memory, her faith—our boundless heritage.

PAPA is carrying on the work he loves. His birthdays show that he has passed the age for active ministry, but his strength and point of view seem ageless. Since there is a preacher shortage, Papa serves a full-time church. Being a shepherd to his flock, comforting those in sorrow, performing marriages, christening babies, filling his pulpit on Sunday, and holding Wednesday-night prayer service, he is still a vital part of the American way of life.

A young grandson visited him one recent Sunday. As they walked home from church, Papa failed to notice the little bundle under Billy's arm, or took it to be his usual Sunday-school papers.

When Papa was settled in his armchair, Billy climbed up into his lap.

"You know somepin', Gran'dad?" he said. "You're the best preacher in the whole world. Your sermons are jus' right!"

"Is that so, Bill?" said Papa, and his chest expanded.

"Yep," said Bill, "I like 'em. They're jus' right. You know why?"

Papa did not know.

"They're jus' ezackly three funny books long!"

Keeping step with modern trends unknowingly, but holding high the same banner, Papa is a preacher still!